cards that pop up, flip & slide

MICHAEL JACOBS

> "the writing will last as
> long as the paper does—
> or longer." (LLOYD REYNOLDS)
> Lloyd preferred cursive
> Italic for lettering, not

> starlight,
> moonlight,
> sunlight
> —and we still
> bump into things

NORTH LIGHT BOOKS
CINCINNATI, OHIO
www.artistsnetwork.com

about the author

michael jacobs is Art Director of The Creative Zone and a full-time artist and instructor who has worked in mixed media and sculpture for over twenty-five years. For eight of those years, he operated a design studio specializing in paper engineering, props and signage.

In 1990, Michael designed and fabricated the world's largest photo album (including 7,500 photos and weighing 228 pounds!) for the Kodak Goodwill Games. He has been creating sculptural books ever since. His artist books, wood and leather objects are displayed in private collections across America, and he teaches papercrafting, book arts and mixed-media sculpture workshops throughout the United States and Canada.

In addition, Michael's work has been published in many books and periodicals, as well as exhibited at the Art Directors Club in New York and in numerous galleries. Michael and Judy Jacobs are co-authors of **Creative Correspondence**, a how-to papercrafting book published by North Light Books. Find out more at their Web site: www.thecreativezone.com.

Editor: Krista Hamilton
Designer: Stephanie Strang
Layout Artist: Jessica Schultz
Production Coordinator: Kristen Heller
Photographers: Tim Grondin, Christine Polomsky and Greg Grosse Photography, Inc. (photos © Greg Grosse)

11 10 09 08 07 9 8 7 6 5

Library of Congress Cataloging-in-Publication Division

Jacobs, Michael
   Cards that pop up, flip & slide / Michael Jacobs.
      p. cm.
   ISBN-13: 978-1-58180-596-3 (pbk. : alk. paper)
   ISBN-10: 1-58180-596-9 (pbk. : alk. paper)
   1. Greeting cards. I. Title

TT872.J33 2005
741.6'84--dc22
                          2004053154

fw
F+W PUBLICATIONS, INC.

metric conversion chart

TO CONVERT	TO	MULTIPLY BY
Inches	Centimeters	2.54
Centimeters	Inches	0.4
Feet	Centimeters	30.5
Centimeters	Feet	0.03
Yards	Meters	0.9
Meters	Yards	1.1
Sq. Inches	Sq. Centimeters	6.45
Sq. Centimeters	Sq. Inches	0.16
Sq. Feet	Sq. Meters	0.09
Sq. Meters	Sq. Feet	10.8
Sq. Yards	Sq. Meters	0.8
Sq. Meters	Sq. Yards	1.2
Pounds	Kilograms	0.45
Kilograms	Pounds	2.2
Ounces	Grams	28.4
Grams	Ounces	0.04

DEDICATION

To my mom, Lucile (with one "L") Jacobs,

who has always been a creative and supportive influence.

To my sister, Mariann (1954–2003),

who loved her secret garden and quiltmaking, and had

a special flair for color, home decor and storytelling.

special thanks

When I develop a new workshop, I design the projects and handouts, and (I hope) control the ebb and flow of the class. How-to books are a collaborative effort. As the author of this book, I had to relinquish control to several people, and this doesn't come easy for me. Nevertheless, I thoroughly enjoyed working with these professionals at North Light Books and found it an exciting learning experience. I want to thank them big-time for the care and expertise they brought to this project:

Krista Hamilton, editor, for her superb job of handling the text and organization.

Christine Polomsky, photographer, whose step-by-step pictures are composed and exposed so clearly.

Stephanie Strang, designer extraordinaire, for her amazing ability to make so much stuff look so visually appealing and yet different from her previous books.

Thank you, Teri Martin and Creative Imaginations, for providing the beautiful scrapbook papers and stickers used for many of the cards and envelopes in this book.

Thank you, Barbara Richards, artist and friend, for turning my handwritten quotes into computer-generated text blocks used on cards throughout this book.

Thank you, students, friends and family for your continued support and encouragement over many years. Words cannot do justice to how much this means to me.

And finally, thank you, Judy, whose love and support have been unwavering and freely given for eighteen years, and whose many talents never cease to amaze me.

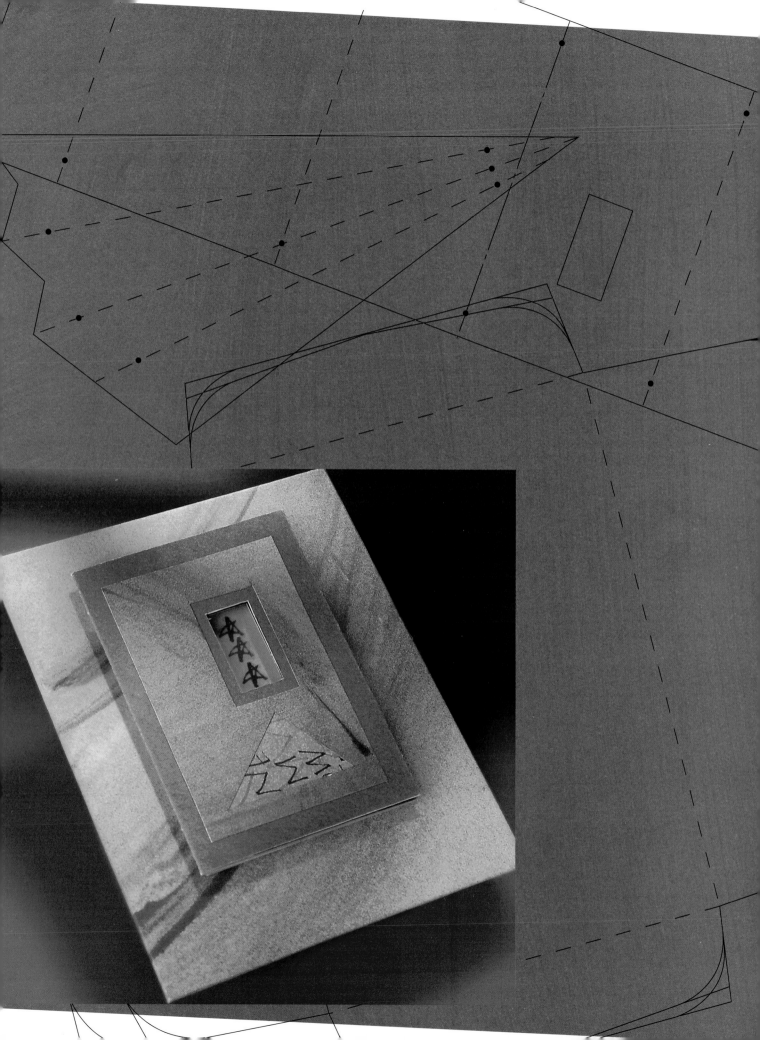

table of contents

intro **duction**

My goal with this book is to show you step-by-step how to make a wide variety of action cards. As you learn the skills and techniques needed to construct the simple cards at the beginning of the book, you will automatically gain confidence for the cards that follow, which are nothing more than simple cards with multiple parts.

Pop-ups are the most common type of action cards. My lifelong fascination with pop-ups began as a child, when my mother brought home my first of many pop-up books. I was mesmerized by the varied mechanisms and spent countless hours pouring over them from all angles, trying to figure out how these magical structures worked.

When I was about eight years old, I asked my mom to save candy, soap, perfume and gift boxes for me. I placed the boxes around my bedroom in groupings that resembled miniature cities.

Hello artists and papercrafters!

Welcome to the exciting world of action cards— interactive greeting cards with movable parts.

My young mind was intrigued by the reality that flat sheets of paper and cardboard could become sturdy, beautiful, three-dimensional boxes. How was it done? I didn't have a clue.

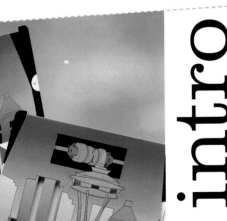

I challenged myself to make sketches of what the boxes would look like opened up and flattened out. My first sketchbooks were filled with many strange and intricate drawings that looked nothing like the opened containers. They were hilarious! By the time I was eleven or so, my drawings had improved considerably, and I started constructing simple boxes. At first, I opened and traced the original boxes, then I designed some of my own, and a few crude pop-ups, too! My career as a paper engineer had begun!

Even today, pop-ups are magical to me, and I still like boxes. I've designed dozens of pop-ups, boxes and other kinds of moveable cards over the years. I make lots of flat drawings and models as I bring the abstract concepts in my head to three-dimensional life. Those models take me back to the tiny cityscapes of my childhood and evoke many pleasant memories.

I hope you enjoy the projects in this book. You are about to "engineer" your way through some exciting action cards. Have fun, enjoy the journey and challenge yourself to create action cards of your own design!

Michael

a 3-D kinda guy

tools and materials

You can create all the action cards in this book with the basic tools shown in the photo below. The additional tools and embellishments in the auxiliary tool kit will turn your action cards into mini works of art.

basic tool kit

CLOCKWISE FROM TOP CENTER: double-sided tape; glue stick; erasers; scoring tool; craft knife and blades; scissors; awl; cutting mat; rulers; bone folders; tweezers; mechanical pencil; Japanese screw punch; utility knife; oval template

The following tools are needed to make the projects in this book.

awl I recommend an awl with a narrow shaft that is the same diameter throughout its length. I find my aluminum-handled awl (used by potters) to be easier to hold than a wooden-handled awl.

bone folder This is used for making a depression in paper or cardstock to help it fold more easily, called scoring. It is also used for creasing and burnishing. For more information, see page 12.

cardstock, mat board and paper Cardstock is a heavy, sturdier paper available in every solid color in the rainbow. Mat board is a heavy-weight cardboard that is great for backing. Decorative paper is light weight and comes in every design imaginable. For many of the cards in this book, I used paper designed by artist Teri Martin. See page 20 for a sampling.

double-sided tape This is excellent for closing envelopes, adhering paper cutouts and assembling pop-up components. Look for double-sided tape on a roll with peel-off backing so you can work with one sticky side at a time. Also, be sure your tape and other supplies are acid-free. Acid breaks down the chemicals in paper and causes it to disintegrate over time.

eraser I recommend using a white vinyl eraser, which removes pencil marks cleanly and with minimal particle buildup. A clickable eraser in a pen-like holder is also good for reaching into tight spots.

glue stick For most of the projects in this book, all you need is a glue stick. I recommend the UHU Stic glue stick, which is acid-free and water-soluble.

hole punches Punches are available in many shapes and sizes. I use a Japanese screw punch, which includes seven interchangeable tips that allow you to "drill" holes anywhere on your paper.

knives Craft knives come in different sizes and are excellent for cutting paper. Utility knives are larger, have heavy-duty blades and work best for cutting cardstock and mat board. Make sure your blade is sharp—dull blades are more likely to cause accidents.

mechanical pencil I recommend using a 0.5mm mechanical pencil with non-smearing 2H lead. This eliminates the need for a sharpener and increases accuracy with crisp, thin lines.

rulers For measuring, buy an architectural ruler with a ⅟₁₆" (1.6mm) scale. For cutting, buy 6" (15.2cm) and 12" (30.5cm) steel rulers with cork backing. For more about rulers, see page 11.

scissors A large and small pair of craft scissors will come in handy for cutting curves; however, it is more accurate to cut straight lines with a knife and ruler.

scoring tool This is used for making valley and mountain scores. For more about scoring tools, see page 12.

self-healing cutting mat A small mat is great for small projects, but if you must settle for one mat, however, a medium or large size is more practical.

templates and french curves These are invaluable for creating circles and ovals for windows, or curves for customized flaps and corners.

tweezers These help with the precise placement of tiny objects.

auxiliary tool kit

Here is just a sampling of the ever-increasing supply of tools and embellishments available for papercrafters. They will greatly increase your creative options.

acrylic and watercolor paints These are available in a huge variety of colors. Clean-up is easy and they are virtually odorless. They are excellent for adhering collage papers or as a protective finish on completed projects.

acrylic matte medium This creates a matte, or flat, finish when mixed with paint and can also be used as a light adhesive for paper.

craft glue Water-soluble craft glue, such as Aleene's Tacky Glue, is excellent for attaching three-dimensional elements. It holds well and dries quickly.

markers and colored pencils My favorite color tool, Primacolor Art Stix, are richly pigmented colored pencils without the wood. I use them flat to fill

in large areas or hold them like a crayon to add squiggles. Double-ended markers with fine and bullet points are also great for drawing, writing messages and adding color.

eyelets and brads These are available in a variety of sizes, shapes and colors, and add dimension to cards. They can be used to attach panels, text blocks and other materials to paper and cardstock. Eyelets are set with a hammer and setting tool. Brad prongs are placed through a slit and bent outward.

inkpads Inkpads are great for adding color to your art. Use them with rubber stamps, or stamp the pad directly onto a card. Dye-based ink is thin, dries fast and cleans up easily. Pigment ink is thicker, does not dry on certain types of paper and resists fading.

molding paste This lightweight, acid-free medium creates a three-dimensional surface texture when applied with a spatula or similar spreading tool. It can be painted with acrylics when dry, or acrylic paint can be mixed into it before application to add color.

rubber stamps These are ideal for use with action cards, and the variety is mind-boggling.

spatula I recommend using a small spatula or putty knife to spread molding paste onto your surface.

thread, ribbon and findings Use these as a collage element or when making cards with woven panels. For more about woven panels, see page 18.

watercolor blocks Each watercolor block consists of twenty sheets of acid-free watercolor paper, which are glued together at the edges. They come in a wide range of sizes and are available in art supply stores. For more about using a watercolor block, see page 17.

CLOCKWISE FROM TOP RIGHT: watercolor block; brads; hammer; eyelet setter; eyelets; craft glue; spatula; gel medium; markers; paintbrushes; gel pens; colored pencils; ribbon; fibers; rubber stamp; ink; paint

All the action cards in this book use the same basic techniques. This section teaches you how to determine the grain direction of your paper and use your tools properly, as well as how to measure, cut, score, fold and crease with precision. I have also included instructions for decorating watercolor blocks, weaving paper, covering a mat board and making a basic easel to display your cards.

getting started

determining grain direction

Machine-made paper, cardstock and mat board all have a grain direction. This simply means that the fibers from which the paper is made lie primarily in one direction. Why is this important? Because paper folded against the grain, or across the direction of the fibers, is weaker, tends to crack and will not lie flat.

The main folds on the cards in this book (and any action cards) will look better and last longer if they run parallel to the grain. Check the materials list to determine whether your project components should be grain short (gs), with the grain running parallel to the short dimension, or grain long (gl), with the grain running parallel to the long dimension. Grain direction specifies the correct direction after you cut your paper, cardstock or mat board.

It is also important to note that all measurements in this book are listed width first, then height. For instance, 9" x 4" (22.9cm x 10.2cm) refers to paper that is 9" (22.9cm) wide and 4" (10.2cm) tall. When working with a square, where the dimensions are the same on all sides, the instructions will specify grain vertical (gv) or grain horizontal (gh), to tell you how to orient your square when you make the card. When the grain direction is not specified, it is irrelevant and can be positioned either way.

The label on a ream of paper or cardstock usually indicates grain direction by underlining the measurement that goes with the grain. To test an individual sheet or board for grain direction, first flex the sheet in one direction, then turn the sheet 90° and flex it again. The sheet will bend easier (offer less resistance) when flexed parallel to the grain. Shown below are two additional methods for determining grain direction: the fold test and the spray test.

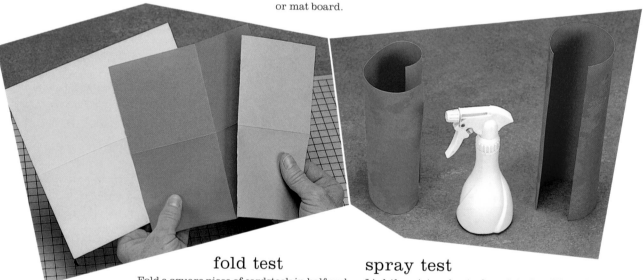

fold test

Fold a square piece of cardstock in half and lightly crease it with your fingertip. Open the cardstock, fold it the other way and lightly crease it again. Open the cardstock and examine the folds. The rough fold runs against the grain and the smooth fold runs parallel to the grain.

spray test

Lightly mist a sheet of cardstock with water. The cardstock will instantly start to curl in the direction of the grain. Imagine grain direction as a tree trunk standing upright inside the curled paper. The blue sheet in this photo is grain short (gs) and the orange sheet is grain long (gl).

using a ruler

When I teach workshops, students often say, "I don't know how to use a ruler." I can see frustration and fear on their faces, and this baffles me. It takes no more time to be precise when measuring and cutting than it does to be sloppy! By mastering the techniques that follow, you will gain the confidence to measure and cut accurately.

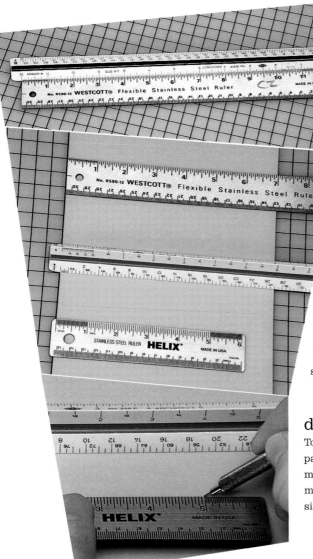

don't switch rulers

Always use the same ruler throughout the construction of a project to minimize measuring discrepancies. The two rulers in the photo to the left are lined up with the zero point on the metal ruler opposite the 12" (30.5cm) point on the white ruler. Look closely at the points on the metal ruler. They do not match up with the points on the white ruler.

align ruler properly

My favorite ruler for measuring is a triangular architectural ruler (center left). Its angled surface has thinner lines than most metal (top left) and plastic (bottom left) rulers, and they rest right on the surface of the paper, so you can accurately transfer measurements to your paper.

When measuring, make sure to properly align the zero point on your ruler with the left edge of the paper, parallel to the top and bottom of the paper. In the photo to the left, the zero point on the metal ruler is at the very end of the ruler, but the zero points on the architectural and plastic rulers are set in from the ends.

draw, score and cut properly

To draw, score or cut a line, measure over from the left edge of your paper and make tick marks with your pencil. Mark your measurements toward the top of your paper first, then use the same ruler to mark the bottom of your paper. The metal ruler can be tilted up to simulate an architectural ruler for greater accuracy.

HELPFUL**HINT**

rulers: which side is up?
The cork on the back of a metal ruler not only keeps it from sliding around, but also raises the edge of the ruler and provides a higher wall to run your tool against. This is a nice safety feature when cutting, however it may cause your pencil, scoring tool or knife to wander underneath the raised edge. To solve this problem, flip your ruler over, holding cork-side up, and use the edge simply as a guide to get straight lines, scores and cuts.

scoring tools

Clean scores and folds, which are often made with bone folders, make all the difference in cardmaking. Ultimately, the thickness at the tip of your tool should be the same as a jumbo paper clip, which is ideal for scoring cardstock and heavy text paper. The steps below demonstrate how to shape your bone folder to function flawlessly, as well as how to make your own scoring tool.

shape your bone folder

Run all sides of the bone folder along 100-grit sandpaper to make them straight. (The lower the grit, the rougher the sandpaper.) Hold the bone folder at an angle and round off the edges. Sand the tip to make a slightly rounded point. Smooth the surface with 150-, 220- and 400-grit sandpaper, then "polish" with 600-grit sandpaper. Soak your shaped and polished bone folder in mineral oil or 30-weight car oil for three to five days, turning it periodically. Rinse with hot, soapy water and dry before using.

make your own scoring tool

Open a jumbo paper clip and snip off about ¾" (1.9cm) of the smaller rounded end with wire cutters. Lightly hammer the cut ends to flatten them. Carefully remove the blade from your craft knife and use pliers to insert the ends of the paper clip into the handle. Tighten firmly.

TRY THIS!

For an antiqued bone folder like the one I am holding in the photo on the left, soak in a mixture of strong coffee grounds and water for a week or so, checking periodically. Remove when it has darkened to your liking, then soak in oil.

scoring, folding and creasing

There are two types of folds: valley folds, which are made by scoring the front (top) of the paper, and mountain folds, which are made by scoring the back (bottom) of the paper. The following steps demonstrate how to achieve crisp, clean folds by making valley and mountain scores.

1 **align ruler**
To make a valley score, mark the placement of your score with tick marks at the top and bottom of your cardstock. Stab the center of the bottom mark with your scoring tool and slide one end of your ruler firmly against the tool, cork-side up. Slide the other end of the ruler to the top mark, then back off just a hair to account for the thickness of your scoring tool.

2 score along tick marks

Hold the ruler firmly in place and run the scoring tool back and forth two or three times against the edge of the ruler. This will compress the fibers of the paper along the intended fold.

3 bend cardstock at score

Slide your bone folder under the cardstock and run it along the edge of the ruler. The cardstock will bend easily along the score to start a crisp, precise fold.

4 crease with bone folder

Remove the ruler, fold the cardstock all the way over at the score and line up the top and bottom edges of the paper. Place a clean sheet of scrap paper over the fold and crease with your bone folder. The scrap paper will prevent the bone folder from leaving shiny marks on the cardstock.

5 mountain score

To make a mountain score, mark the placement of your score with tick marks on the front of the cardstock, and use an awl to pierce the holes. Flip the cardstock over and line your ruler up on the pierced holes. Score, fold and crease as you did in steps 1–4.

HELPFUL**HINT**

Some of the photos throughout the book show me creasing and burnishing, or smoothing, paper and cardstock without covering it with scrap paper. These are for visual purposes only. Always cover your surface with scrap paper before you crease or burnish. This will prevent your tools from leaving shiny marks on your paper.

6 examine folds

The scored, folded and creased cardstock shown to the right has four valley folds and three mountain folds.

cutting out stencils and interior windows

Crisply cut windows and stencils give cards a more geometric look. This cutting technique creates stencils and interior windows with crisp corners and no overcutting.

1 draw and cut lines

Draw or trace the shape onto your paper or cardstock. Stab your knife blade into the upper-left corner of the window. Swing your ruler gently into the knife blade and align it with the pencil line. Cut along the line, stopping just short of the bottom corner. Remove your knife and repeat the cutting process on the remaining lines, stopping just short of the corner with each cut.

2 stab corners

Flip the paper over and lightly stab each attached corner with your knife, aligning the blade with the previous cut. This stabbing action slices through the tiny bit of paper left at each corner.

using a half pattern

Any of the half patterns in this book can be made into symmetrical whole patterns, as shown here. Using a half pattern ensures that both sides of the shape are symmetrical.

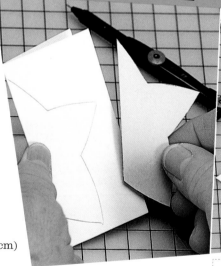

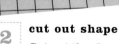

1 score cardstock and trace pattern

Position a 4" x 4" (10.2cm x 10.2cm) piece of cardstock grain vertical (gv). Measure over 2" (5.1cm) from the left edge, valley score, fold and crease the cardstock. (For instructions, see pages 12–13.) Place the edge indicated on the pattern flush against the fold of the cardstock and trace the pattern.

2 cut out shape

Cut out the shape through both layers of cardstock. Open the cardstock to reveal a whole, symmetrical pattern.

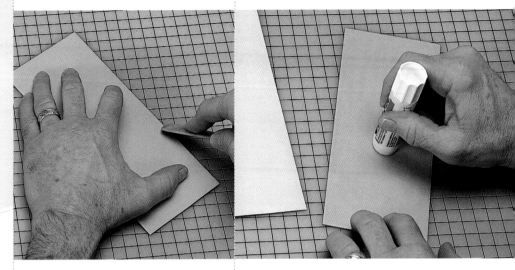

covering a mat board

Mat board, or heavy-weight cardboard, creates a sturdy mounting surface, as well as a beautiful background for a card. The following steps demonstrate how to cover a #10 size board, but I have also included materials for covering an A-2 size board.

materials >>

#10 board

#10 board > 3¾" x 9" (9.5cm x 22.9cm) mat board (grain long)

#10 cover paper > 5¼" x 10½" (13.3cm x 26.7cm) piece of decorative paper (grain long)

#10 liner > 3¼" x 8½" (8.3cm x 21.6cm) piece of decorative paper (grain long)

basic tool kit (page 8)

a-2 board

a-2 board > 4" x 5" (10.2cm x 12.7cm) mat board (grain long)

a-2 cover paper > 5½" x 6¾" (14cm x 17.1cm) piece of decorative paper (grain long)

a-2 liner > 3¾" x 4¾" (9.5cm x 12.1cm) piece of decorative paper (grain long)

basic tool kit (page 8)

1 round edges of board

Place the mat board in the vertical position. Run the blunt end of your bone folder at an angle along all four edges of the board three or four times, applying firm pressure. Flip the board over and repeat. This process compresses the fibers along the edges of the board and rounds them slightly, making the board easier to cover.

2 adhere board to cover paper

Place the cover paper face-down on your work surface. Run the glue stick over one side of the mat board and adhere it to the paper, centered top to bottom and left to right.

3 burnish

Flip the mat board over and place a clean piece of scrap paper over the cover paper. Work your bone folder outward from the center to spread the glue evenly across the board and smooth the surface. This is called burnishing.

HELPFUL**HINT**

Glue sticks tend to get soft and mushy in hot or humid weather. Keep one glue stick in your refrigerator and one at your work station, and switch off when necessary for hassle-free gluing!

4 cut off corners

Flip the mat board over again and cut off the corners of the cover paper, about ⅛" (0.3cm) from the corners of the board. You will be left with four flaps of cover paper.

5 curve in flaps

Curve all four flaps around the board by sliding each side of the board against your work surface in a semi-circular motion. This will make it easier to glue down the flaps.

6 glue and tuck opposite flaps

Hold the glue stick against one of the long sides of the board and run it over the flap. Fold the flap over and pull it snugly toward the center of the board with your fingertips. Burnish with your bone folder through scrap paper. While the glue is still moist, use the tip of your bone folder to tuck the corners of the flap around the ends of the board as shown. Repeat the gluing and tucking process with the opposite flap.

7 glue down remaining flaps

Glue down one of the two remaining flaps and burnish with your bone folder. While the glue is still moist, use the flat side of your bone folder to wrap the short length of paper at each corner around the long side of the board. Repeat with the opposite flap.

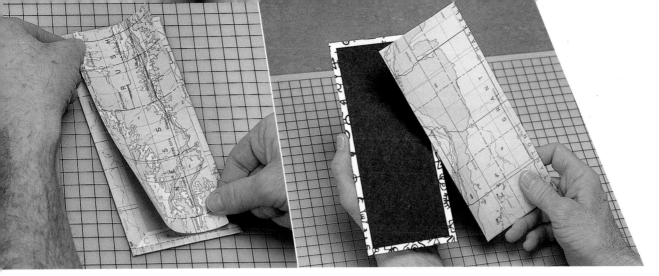

8 adhere liner

Apply glue to the inside surface of the liner paper, adhere it to the center of the uncovered side of the board and burnish.

CHALLENGE!

For a consistent look on both sides of the mat board, cover the front and back with the same decorative paper (above right). For a striking contrast, line the board with a solid-color paper (above left).

using a watercolor block

Watercolor blocks, found in art supply stores, make working with watercolor paper fun and easy. They can be soaked and worked repeatedly, and they always dry flat. Each watercolor block consists of twenty acid-free sheets of watercolor paper that is glued together at the edges. They range from postcard size to 18" x 24" (45.7cm x 61cm), and are available in a variety of finishes, textures and weights. This demonstration shows one of the many ways to use watercolor blocks for decorating cards.

1 decorate top piece

Spray the top sheet of the watercolor block with water and allow it to soak in. Apply paint, ink and molding paste with a spatula or putty knife while the sheet is still damp. Adhere papers with matte medium and add more texture with molding paste. Continue to work in layers, both wet and dry, as desired. When the collage is complete, slide a craft knife into the slit at the back of the watercolor block and remove the top sheet of watercolor paper.

2 cut out squares and rectangles

Cut the collaged sheet of watercolor paper into square and rectangular panels and glue them to the front of your cards, as shown in the photo on the right. (I applied a Teri Martin sticker to the bottom of the rectangle on this card.) Or, score the panels down the middle and use them as your actual cards.

17

Woven panels are a great way to use up extra scraps of decorative paper. They are quick and easy to make, and they add color and texture to your cards. This technique is demonstrated using a basic A-2 card, but you can adapt your panel to fit a #10 card by simply making the paper strips longer.

materials >>

card > basic a-2 or #10 card

woven panel > approximately twenty $^3/_8$" x 6" (1cm x 15cm) paper strips cut or torn parallel to the grain

backing > 5" x 3$^3/_4$" (12.7cm x 9.5cm) piece of cardstock (grain long)

window frame > 5" x 3$^3/_4$" (12.7cm x 9.5cm) piece of plain or decorative paper or cardstock (grain long)

basic tool kit (see page 8)

ribbon, fibers and other embellishments (optional)

TRYTHIS!

Tear the window opening and the outer edges of your window frame, add a quote sticker and glue the frame to the front as shown at the top of the photo.

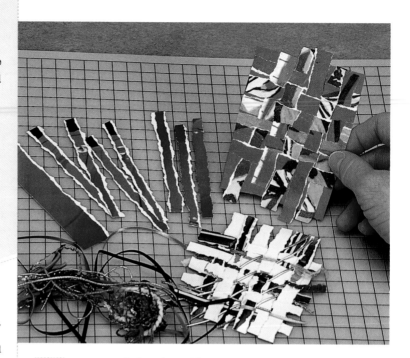

1 **weave strips together**
Weave the paper strips together, adding elements such as ribbon and fibers, if desired. Glue the backing piece to the woven panel to make it sturdier.

2 **prepare window**
Draw or trace a shape onto the front of the window frame paper. Cut or tear out the window and erase any pencil lines. Glue the window frame over the woven panel and trim the panel if necessary. Glue the woven panel and window to the front of an A-2 or #10 card. Burnish.

Easels are so versatile. They can be decorated and sent in A-2 or #10 envelopes as cards, or they can be attached to the back of any card to make it stand up. Cut a window in the front of your easel to highlight your signature, additional text, stamped images or photographs.

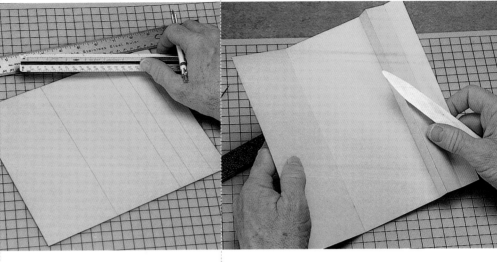

materials >>

card > basic a-2 or #10 card

easel > 10¼" x 8½" (26cm x 21.6cm) piece of cardstock (grain short)

basic tool kit (page 8)

1 **draw vertical lines**
Position the cardstock in the horizontal position. Measure over 3¾" (9.5cm), 7⅜" (18.7cm), 8¼" (21cm) and 9⅜" (23.8cm) from the left edge and draw vertical lines from top to bottom.

2 **score and crease**
Valley score, fold and crease the first, second and fourth lines. Mountain score, fold and crease the third line. (For instructions, see pages 12–13.) The cardstock now has five panels.

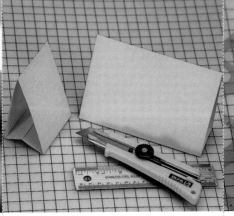

3 **fold, glue and burnish**
Fold panel three to the left, then fold panels four and five to the right. Next, fold panel one to the right. Apply glue to panel five and fold it to the left, over panel one. Burnish.

4 **make two easels**
Decorate the basic easel and send it in a #10 envelope, or cut it into sections to create two or more shorter easels, as shown above.

5 **attach easel to card**
To attach an easel to an A-2 (shown) or #10 card, flatten the easel and apply glue to either side. (The longer side creates the greater angle.) Center the easel on the back of the card with the bottom fold flush with the bottom of the card. Burnish.

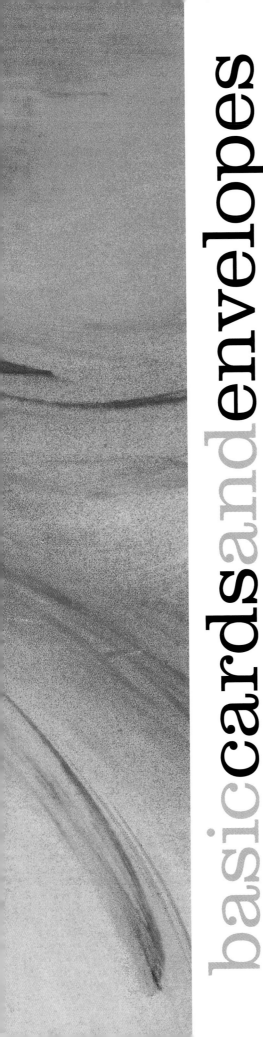

basiccardsandenvelopes

This section shows you how to make the basic cards and envelopes featured in this book. First, you will learn how to make basic A-2 and #10 cards with and without flaps. These are basic components of many of the projects in this book. Then you will learn how to make basic A-2, A-2 button tie and #10 envelopes. All the action cards in this book fit into one of these three envelopes, except for the Shaker Card on page 74, which has its own special mailing wrapper.

A-2 envelopes, which measure $4\frac{3}{8}$" x $5\frac{3}{4}$" (11.1cm x 14.6cm), and #10 envelopes, which measure $4\frac{1}{8}$" x $9\frac{1}{2}$" (10.5cm x 24.1cm), can be mailed at the basic letter rate, as long as the total weight including the card is one ounce or less. (The Shaker Card will require additional postage due to its thickness.) If you design your own action cards, or plan to adapt any of the cards in this book to a different size or shape, I highly recommend asking your local post office for a list of standard rates and dimensions.

For more information, visit these Web sites:

United States: www.usps.com
United Kingdom: www.consignia-online.com
Canada: www.canadapost.ca

This card is designed to fit snugly inside a basic A-2 envelope. A single piece of 8½" x 11" (21.6cm x 27.9cm) cardstock makes two cards with no paper left over. The steps below demonstrate how to make a basic A-2 card, as well as an A-2 card with a full or partial flap.

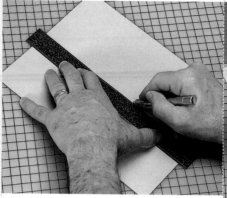
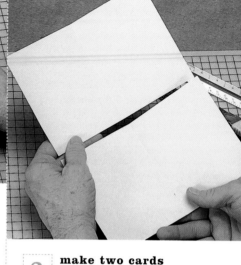

materials >>

two basic a-2 cards > 8½" x 11" (21.6cm x 27.9cm) piece of cardstock (grain long)

full flap > 5½" x 4⅞" (14cm x 12.4cm) piece of cardstock (grain long)

partial flap > 5½" x 3¼" (14cm x 8.3cm) piece of cardstock (grain long)

basic tool kit (page 8)

1 score, fold and crease cardstock

Position the 8½" x 11" (21.6cm x 27.9cm) cardstock in the vertical position. Make tick marks 4¼" (10.8cm) from the left edge of the cardstock, near the top and bottom. Align your ruler on the marks and valley score down the center of the cardstock. Fold and crease. (For instructions, see pages 12–13.)

2 make two cards

Open the cardstock and make tick marks 5½" (14cm) down from the top, near the left and right edges. Align your ruler on the marks and cut the cardstock in half to create two A-2 cards.

3 prepare flaps

To create flaps, place the paper face-down in the vertical position. Measure ¾" (1.9cm) over from the left edge, valley score, fold and crease. In this photo, I am creasing a full flap. The partial flap (left) will be attached in step 5.

4 attach full flap

To attach the full flap, run your glue stick over the inside of narrow panel on the flap. Position an A-2 card face-down with the open end of the card pointing toward the flap fold. Fold the narrow panel into the inside of the card's front flap and burnish.

5 attach partial flap

To attach a partial flap to your card, repeat step 4 with the partial flap cardstock and another A-2 card. You now have basic A-2 cards with full (left) and partial (right) flaps.

The #10 card is just the right size for the basic #10 envelope. Step 1 demonstrates how to make a #10 card with or without flaps. Steps 2 and 3 demonstrate how to add colorful layers to a basic #10 card.

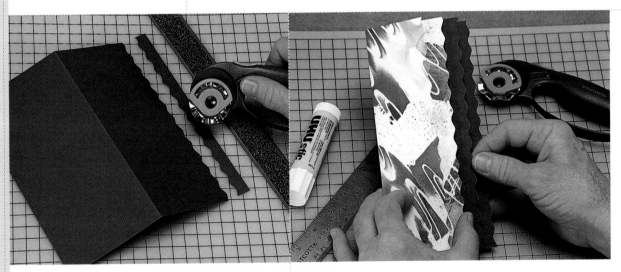

materials >>

basic #10 card > 8" x 8½" (20.3cm x 21.6cm) piece of cardstock (grain long)

full flap > 4½" x 8½" (11.4cm x 21.6cm) piece of cardstock (grain long)

partial flap > 3¾" x 8½" (9.5cm x 21.6cm) piece of cardstock (grain long)

basic tool kit (page 8)

1 prepare basic #10 cards with and without flaps

To make a #10 card (above left), position the 8" x 8½" (20.3cm x 21.6cm) cardstock in the vertical position. Measure over 4" (10.2cm) from the left, valley score, fold and crease. To attach a full (above center) or partial (above right) flap, position the flap cardstock face-down in the vertical position. Measure over ¾" (1.9cm), valley score, fold and crease. Attach the flap to the basic #10 cards as directed on page 22, steps 3 and 4.

2 prepare basic #10 card for layers

Open the basic #10 card and place it face-up with the fold in the vertical position. Cut ½" (1.3cm) from the right edge of the card, using decorative scissors or cutters if desired.

3 add multiple layers

Run your glue stick over the inside surface of the ¾" (1.9cm) panel on a partial flap. Place the fold on your #10 card from step 2 into the fold on the flap. Burnish the ¾" (1.9cm) panel to the back of the card. Cut out and glue additional flaps (layers) in place over the first flap and trim them to the desired width. (I made the vibrant watercolor paper layers on the card in this photo from paper painted by Maggie Gillikin.)

The A-2 envelope pattern on page 25 provides a variety of straight and curved lines at the top, bottom and sides. Photocopy the pattern to cardstock several times, then choose any combination of lines to create patterns with different flap shapes, including asymmetrical flaps on the same envelope, as demonstrated here.

materials >>

envelope > 8½" x 11" (21.6cm x 27.9cm) piece of decorative paper or cardstock

basic a-2 envelope pattern (page 25)

basic tool kit (page 8)

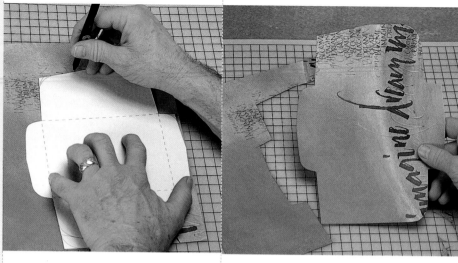

1 **trace pattern onto paper**
Trace the basic A-2 envelope pattern to the decorative side of your envelope paper. This allows you to move the pattern around for the best placement.

2 **cut out envelope**
Cut out the envelope, using a craft knife and ruler for straight lines and scissors for curved lines.

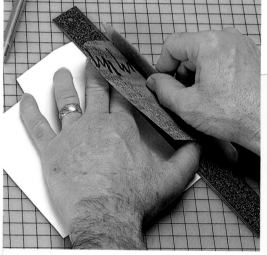

3 **score and crease**
With the decorative side of the envelope face-down, valley score, fold and crease as indicated on the pattern. (For instructions, see pages 12–13.)

HELPFUL**HINT**

Since all envelopes have two scores running with the grain and two running against it, grain direction is irrelevant.

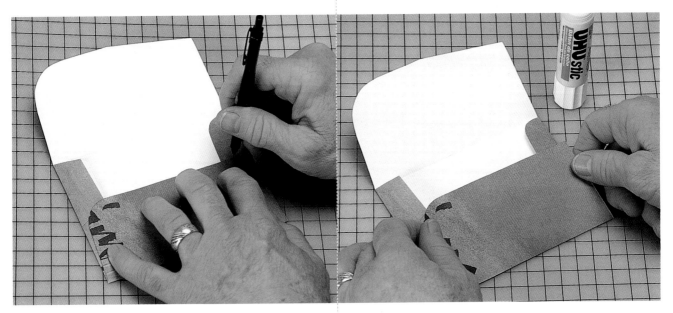

4 **fold and trace flaps**
Fold the side flaps in and the bottom flap up. Trace the edges of the bottom flap to the side flaps.

5 **glue up flaps**
Unfold the bottom flap and apply glue to the traced areas on the side flaps. Use a scrap of paper as a "glue guard" to cover the areas that you do not wish to glue. Fold the bottom flap up and burnish with your bone folder to adhere the bottom flap to the side flaps.

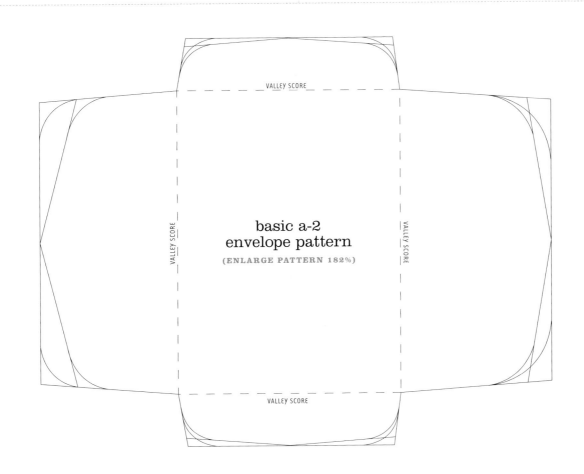

VALLEY SCORE

VALLEY SCORE

VALLEY SCORE

basic a-2
envelope pattern
(ENLARGE PATTERN 182%)

VALLEY SCORE

The basic A-2 button tie envelope is the same size as the basic A-2 envelope; however, the cardstock buttons and string add visual interest and allow the envelope to be used again!

materials >>

envelope > 8½" x 11" (21.6cm x 27.9cm) piece of decorative paper or cardstock

buttons > two 2" x 3" (5.1cm x 7.6cm) scrap pieces of cardstock

button cover > 2" x 3" (5.1cm x 7.6cm) piece of decorative paper

basic a-2 button tie envelope pattern (page 28)

brads

string

basic tool kit (page 8)

1 cut, score, fold and crease envelope

Trace the pattern to the envelope cardstock or paper. Use an awl to pierce holes through the dots indicated on the pattern. Remove the pattern and cut out the envelope. With the decorative side face-down, valley score, fold and crease the envelope as indicated on the pattern.

2 glue cardstock together

Glue two pieces of scrap cardstock back to back, then glue a piece of decorative paper to one side of the scrap cardstock. Burnish.

3 cut out buttons

Use a shape template or draw two button shapes approximately 1¼" (3.2cm) in diameter on the decorative paper. Cut them out with a craft knife or scissors. Buttons can be whatever shape you desire.

4 cut slits in flaps and buttons

Place the envelope decorative-side down with the small flap at the bottom, as shown above. Using the holes you pierced in step 1 as your guide, cut a vertical slit in the top flap and a horizontal slit in the left flap. The slits should be just long enough to accommodate your brad prongs. Cut corresponding horizontal and vertical slits in each button.

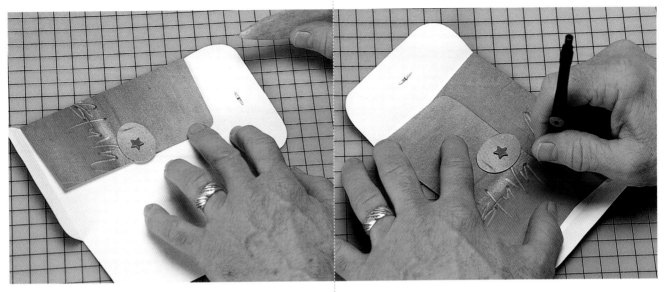

5 **attach buttons**

Use the brads to attach the buttons to the flaps. Bend the prongs outward and flatten them with the pointed end of your bone folder.

6 **trace button flap**

Fold in the right side flap, then fold the left button flap over it. Lightly trace the edge of the left flap to the right flap.

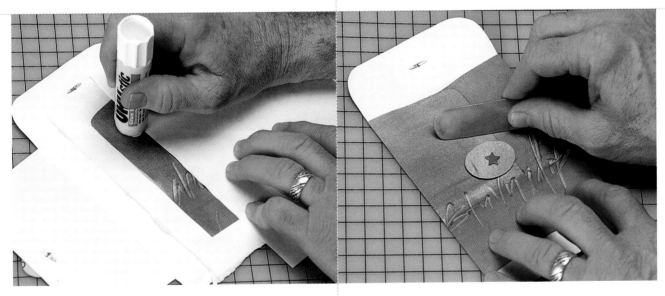

7 **glue up flap**

Open the left flap and apply glue inside the traced area on the right flap, using a glue guard to mask the areas you do not wish to glue.

8 **fold and burnish side flaps**

Fold the left flap back over the right flap and burnish with your bone folder.

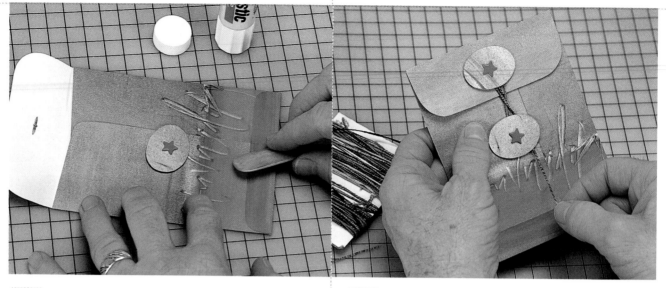

9 **fold and burnish bottom flap**
Apply glue to the inside surface of the bottom flap, fold it up and adhere it to the bottom of the side flaps. Burnish.

10 **tie with string**
Tie a 12" (30.5cm) piece of string behind the button on the top flap. Wind the string around both buttons several times to hold the envelope closed.

HELPFUL**HINT**

To hide the brad prongs and stiffen the top flap, line the inside surface of the flap with decorative paper.

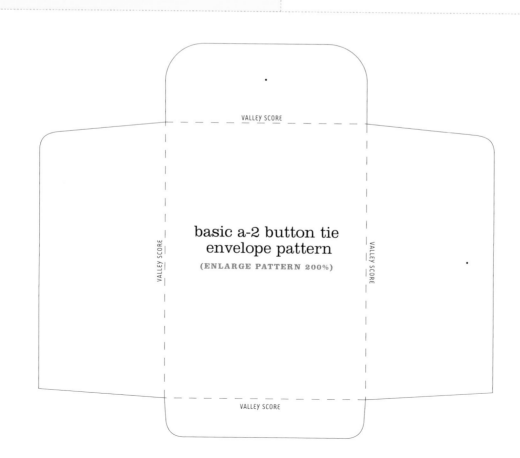

VALLEY SCORE

VALLEY SCORE

VALLEY SCORE

basic a-2 button tie
envelope pattern
(ENLARGE PATTERN 200%)

VALLEY SCORE

The basic #10 envelope
is easy to make in three
simple steps. Follow
these steps to make and
decorate your own.

materials >>

envelope > 12" x 12"
(30.5cm x 30.5cm) piece of
decorative paper or cardstock

basic #10 envelope pattern
(below)

basic tool kit (page 8)

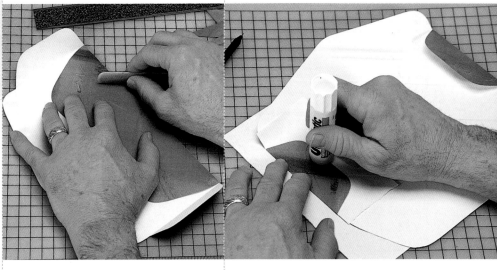

1 cut, score, fold and crease envelope

Trace the pattern to the envelope
cardstock or paper and cut it out.
With the decorative side face-down,
valley score, fold and crease the
envelope as indicated on the pattern.
(For instructions, see pages 12–13.)

2 trace and glue flaps

Position the envelope with the
large flap at the bottom. Fold the side
flaps in, then fold the bottom flap up.
Trace the bottom flap onto the side
flaps. Unfold the bottom flap and
apply glue to the traced areas on
the side flaps, using glue guards to
protect areas you do not wish to glue.
Re-fold the bottom flap and burnish.

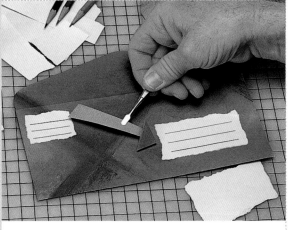

3 adhere address label

Tear or cut address labels from scrap
paper. Glue it in place and burnish. Add address
lines with colored pencils and markers, and
decorate the envelope as desired.

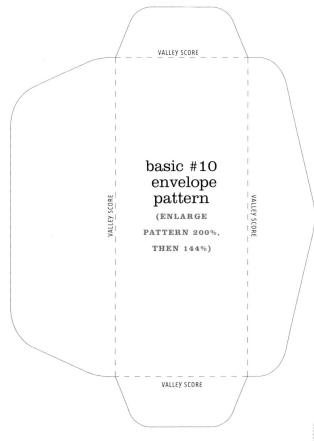

VALLEY SCORE

VALLEY SCORE

VALLEY SCORE

basic #10 envelope pattern

(ENLARGE
PATTERN 200%,
THEN 144%)

VALLEY SCORE

action cards

To me, action cards are gifts in and of themselves. It is exciting to open a card and see a three-dimensional shape emerge from the fold, or to pull a tab and have an image or word magically appear in a window. Action cards can be tailor-made to fit any occasion, and the recipient will be honored to know you took the time to make the card yourself.

The recipient is not the only one to benefit here. Learning to use your tools as you construct these action cards will improve your own hand-eye coordination, enhance your spatial awareness and increase your ability to solve problems!

The action cards that follow are arranged with the simpler ones at the beginning. If you are new to papercrafting or cardmaking, start with these cards. By following the simple step-by-step instructions, you will become familiar with the basic skills and techniques needed to make all the other cards. Measuring, cutting and scoring will become second nature as you learn how to construct the different mechanisms. As you complete these action cards, you will become more aware of the amazing three-dimensional world around you!

So turn the page, grab your tools, roll up your sleeves and get started making these captivating marvels of paper engineering.

Almost ten years ago, as Artist-in-Action for King County Solid Waste, I taught workshops on creative ways to re-use paper. At the end of one workshop, a student named Alice Hammond showed me bookmarks she had made from used envelopes. I have since passed the idea on to scores of students. The cost is zilch and the possibilities are endless. Another student, Sherry Laatsch, taught children how to make them in her library classes with the theme "Whales, scales and fishy tales." She sent me three of the bookmarks pictured below, and I used her idea for this step-by-step bookmark project.

bookmark
card

materials >>

card > basic a-2 card with or without flap

liner > 3½" x 5" (8.9cm x 12.7cm) piece of decorative paper or cardstock (grain long)

used envelope

rubber stamps, inks, colored pencils, markers and other decorating supplies

basic tool kit (page 8)

1 draw design

Draw a design in the bottom right corner of a used envelope. Decorate the design with rubber stamps, colored pencils, markers and other decorating supplies. Save the bottom left corner of the envelope to make another bookmark later.

2 cut out bookmark

Use scissors to cut out the bookmark and trim off all but the small corner section on the back of the envelope. This will be the tab that holds the bookmark on the corner of the page.

3 trace corner to card

Position the bookmark on the right panel of the opened A-2 card near the center and trace the corner. Cut along these lines with your knife to make a right angle slit. Slip the bookmark tab onto the slit. It will appear to be floating on the card. (Artist Jane Shibata came up with the idea for hanging the bookmark on a card.)

4 attach liner

To finish the card, run your glue stick around the edges of the liner paper. Center it on the back of the A-2 card and burnish.

star bookmark

This star of David bookmark was based on one by Barbi Striar Disraelly. To make this bookmark, cut out two equilateral triangles. Cut a slit in one triangle and slide one point from the other triangle through the slit. Glue them together to form a star. Then, glue the star to the corner of a used envelope and cut out as shown.

<<

candle bookmark

Barbi Striar Disraelly also designed and created this lively birthday card and candle bookmark. The text and candle really complement each other.

>>

Many dress Birthday Cakes
with one candle to represent each year
and one to "grow on"
or one for "good luck"

In our family's tradition
I send you this candle to "wish on":

May
your Birthday
be all you wish for ...

May
your wishes
all come true ...

And ....
May your first wish
be for PEACE

Hugs and Ciaobiddy

barbi@darius.co.il

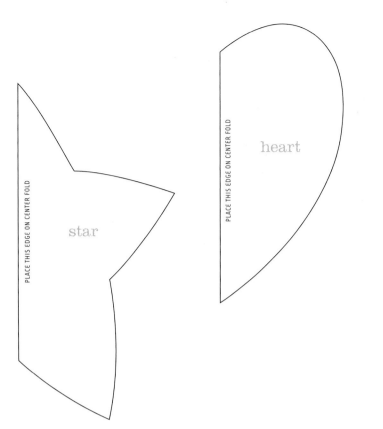

PLACE THIS EDGE ON CENTER FOLD

star

PLACE THIS EDGE ON CENTER FOLD

heart

PLACE THIS EDGE ON CENTER FOLD

shamrock

bookmark card patterns

(SHOWN AT ACTUAL SIZE)

For more about how to use
a half pattern, see page 14.

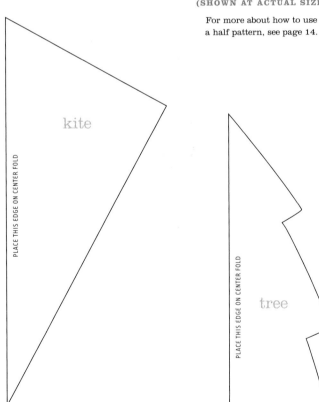

PLACE THIS EDGE ON CENTER FOLD

kite

PLACE THIS EDGE ON CENTER FOLD

tree

PLACE THIS EDGE ON CENTER FOLD

butterfly

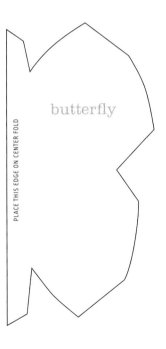

The V-fold is perhaps the most common and versatile mechanism used in commercial pop-ups. V-folds make it easy to create pop-ups with a huge range of movement and effects. The butterfly in the card pictured below has a full 90° arc and hovers outside the top of the opened card. The other half patterns on page 35 work with this Simple V Card, too!

simple v
card

materials >>

card > a-2 card with partial flap

pop-up mechanism > 8" x 5" (20.3cm x 12.7cm) piece of cardstock (grain short)

butterfly > 3½" x 3½" (8.9cm x 8.9cm) piece of decorative paper or cardstock

liners > scraps of decorative paper (optional)

butterfly pattern (page 35)

basic tool kit (page 8)

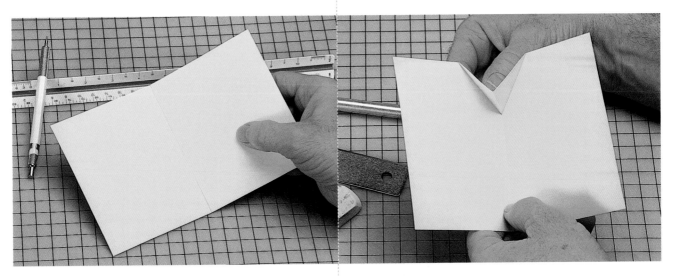

1 score, crease and fold cardstock

Position the pop-up mechanism cardstock in the horizontal position. Measure over 4" (10.2cm) from the left edge and valley score vertically down the center. Fold and crease the cardstock. (For instructions, see pages 12–13.) Draw a dot on the fold 1½" (3.8cm) from the top. Then, measure 1½" (3.8cm) to the left and right of the center fold and draw dots at the top edge of the cardstock.

2 make v-fold

Valley score the V-shape formed by the dots. Erase all remaining pencil lines. Push the V inward to invert it toward the center as you close the cardstock. Crease the folds.

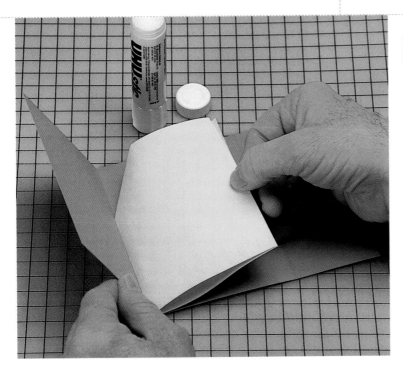

3 attach mechanism to card

Apply glue to the back right panel of the cardstock and insert it into the center fold of the A-2 card with the V-fold at the top. Close the card and burnish. Re-open the card and apply glue to the back left panel of the card-stock. Close the card and burnish again.

TRYTHIS!

To make your image pop "down," glue the card-stock to the card with the V-fold at the bottom.

4 | position butterfly

Trace the butterfly pattern from page 35 to decorative paper or cardstock and cut it out. (For instructions on how to use a half pattern, see page 14.) Glue or tape the butterfly to one side of the V-fold. Play around with the placement of the butterfly before gluing to make sure it fits completely inside the card when it is closed. Close the card and burnish.

5 | line card

To finish the card, cut out liners slightly smaller than the panels on your card and glue them to the inside of the card. Trim if necessary and add a message.

CHALLENGE!

To embellish your card even further, cut out and glue a body to the butterfly. Glue additional butterflies to the card and envelope, as well.

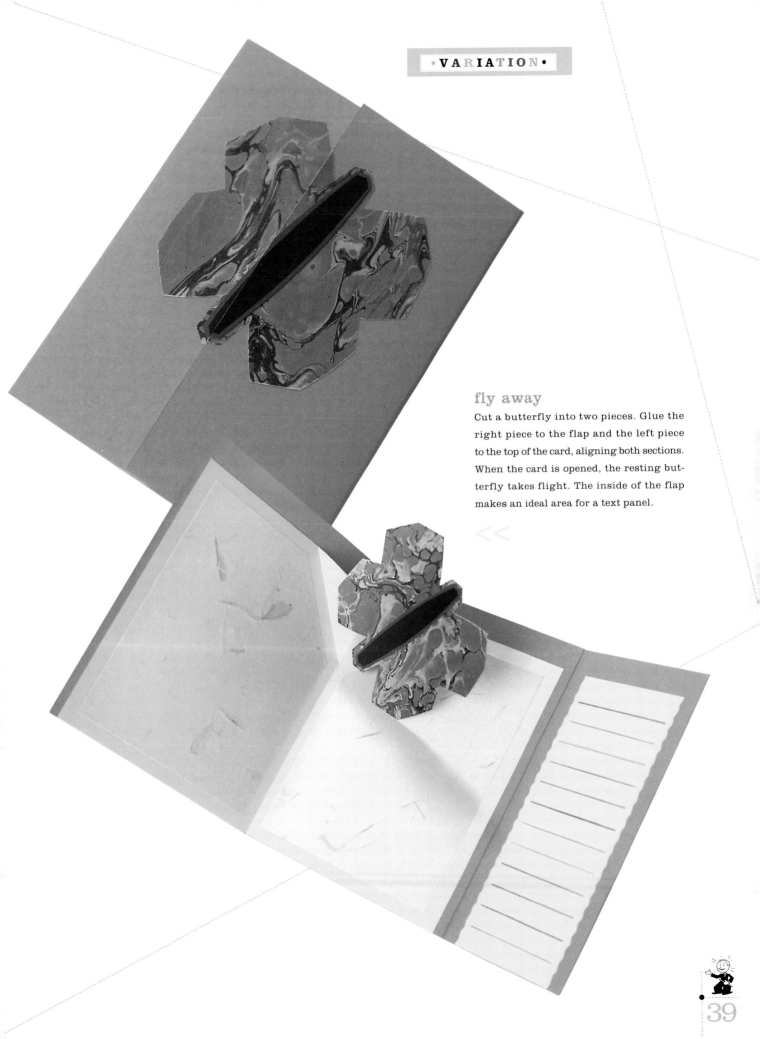

fly away

Cut a butterfly into two pieces. Glue the right piece to the flap and the left piece to the top of the card, aligning both sections. When the card is opened, the resting butterfly takes flight. The inside of the flap makes an ideal area for a text panel.

<<

This card fits nicely into a basic #10 envelope. The pop-up riser can be shaped like a house, arrow, hand, mountain, umbrella, sign, tower, birdhouse or even birthday candles, as shown below. Put on your creativity cap and make the riser pop up from the left side of the card. And, yes, the components can be sized to fit an A-2 card as well!

side-pull v
card

materials >>

card > 11" x 7½" (27.9cm x 19.1cm) piece of cardstock (grain short)

riser > 3" x 5½" (7.6cm x 14cm) piece of cardstock (grain long)

stiffeners > two 7¾" x 2½" (19.7cm x 6.4cm) pieces of cardstock (grain long)

stickers, stamps and other decorating supplies

basic tool kit (page 8)

1 **draw lines on cardstock**

Place the cardstock for the card in the horizontal position. Measure 3¾" (9.5cm) down from the top and lightly draw a horizontal line from side to side. Then, measure 2" (5.1cm) and 3¼" (8.3cm) over from the left edge and draw two vertical lines from top to bottom.

2 **make front and back sections**

Mountain score the 2" (5.1cm) line and valley score the 3¼" (8.3cm) line. Fold and crease each score. (For instructions, see pages 12–13.) Cut the cardstock in half on the horizontal line to create two identical components for the front and back of the card.

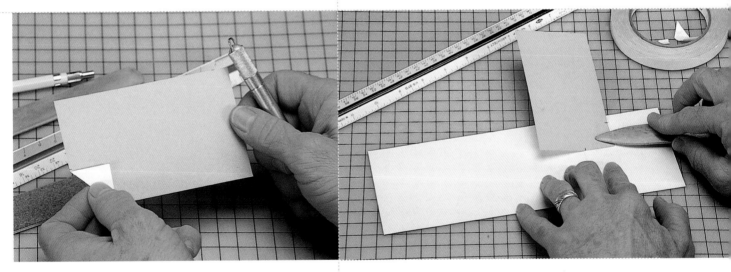

3 **prepare riser**

Place the cardstock for the riser in the horizontal position. Measure over 1⅛" (1.1cm) and up 1⅛" (1.1cm) from the bottom left corner and mark with a pencil. Valley score, fold and crease the diagonal line connecting the marks to make a triangle.

4 **attach riser to back of card**

Place one of the components from step 2 (this will be the back of the card) face-down with the folds on the right side. (The mountain fold will be closer to the right edge than the valley fold.) Apply glue or double-sided tape to the back surface of the triangle on the riser. Attach the riser to the cardstock component, with the triangle centered between the folds and the upper right corner of the triangle ⅜" (1cm) from the top edge. Make sure the long sides of the riser are parallel to the folds. Burnish the triangle.

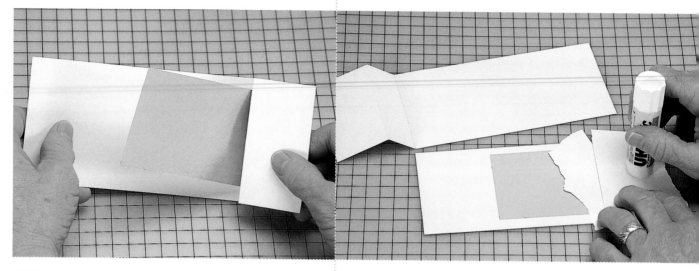

5 fold riser and back of card

Fold the riser down so that the top is pointing to the right. Fold the valley fold of the cardstock component to the left, then fold the mountain fold to the right.

6 glue front and back of card together

Place the remaining component from step 2 (this will be the front of the card) above the back component with the folds on the left side. (The mountain fold will be closer to the left edge than the valley fold.) Apply glue to the right panel on the back component, using glue guards to protect the areas you do not wish to glue.

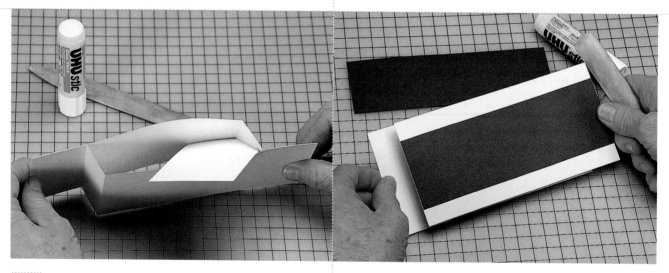

7 attach components

Fold the valley fold of the front component to the right, then fold the mountain fold to the left. Apply glue to the left panel of the front component, using glue guards. Flip the front component over and adhere it to the back component. Burnish the ends of the card over the glued areas. Pull the ends of the card in opposite directions to reveal the pop-up riser.

8 adhere stiffeners

To stiffen the card, glue the cardstock stiffener pieces to the front and back of the card, centered top to bottom. Burnish.

9 add triangles

Glue small triangles to the right and left sides of the card to hint at how the card is operated.

10 decorate card

To finish the card, add text or images to the riser and decorate the front and back of the card with stickers, stamps and other supplies as desired.

TRY THIS!

Glue a pocket (made from a recycled envelope, of course) to the riser to hold a special surprise.

VARIATION

party time

Cut a window in the front of your Side-Pull V Card to expose part of the image or text on the pop up riser (shown above). When the sides are pulled to activate the riser, the window moves to the right and can frame additional text!

The Pedestal Card pop-up mechanism has two V-folds. The V-fold at the top holds an image and the V-fold at the base causes the pedestal to move up and down 150° when the card is opened and closed. You can change the angle at the bottom of the pedestal for greater (or lesser) movement, or cut two shorter pedestals into the fold of the card and have two images pop up! In the card below, I glued a tiny card with the word "Yo!" to the top of the pedestal. I replaced the card with a kite in the step-by-step instructions.

pedestal
card

materials >>

card > #10 card with partial or full flap

spine wrap > 8½" x 2½" (21.6cm x 6.4cm) piece of cardstock (grain long)

kite > 4¼" x 4¼" (10.8cm x 10.8cm) piece of plain or decorative paper

pedestal pattern (page 47)

kite pattern (page 35)

basic tool kit (page 8)

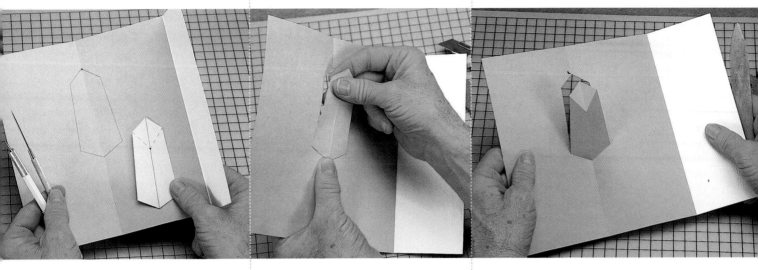

1 trace pattern to card

Open the #10 card and place it in the vertical position with the flap pointing right. Measure 1¼" (3.2cm) down from the top and make a dot on the center fold of the card. Cut out the pedestal pattern and align the point and center line on the pattern with the dot and fold on the card. Trace around the pattern and pierce a hole through the dot.

2 cut out pedestal

Starting at the bottom left corner of the traced pedestal, cut around both sides, leaving the bottom V intact.

3 score and crease pedestal

Valley score from the pierced hole to the upper left and right corners of the pedestal. Then, valley score the bottom, uncut V. (For instructions, see pages 12–13.) Gently push the pedestal forward as you close the card. Crease the folds through the closed card.

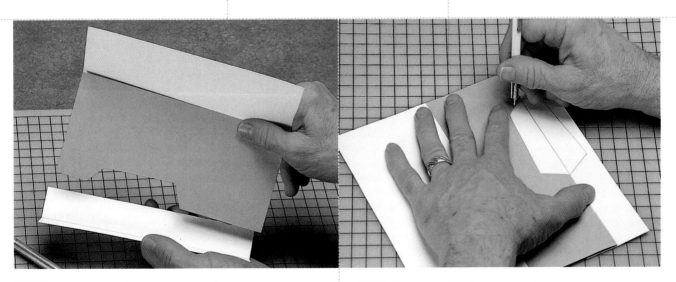

4 prepare spine wrap

Place the spine wrap cardstock face-down in the vertical position. Valley score, fold and crease it down the center. Place the center fold of the closed card into the fold of the spine wrap, flush at the top and bottom. The spine wrap will conceal the cut-out on the side of the card. Place the card and spine wrap on your work surface.

5 trace pedestal cut-out

Open the top flap of the spine wrap to the left and trace the pedestal cut-out from the card onto the spine wrap. Close the top flap and flip the card over. Open the spine wrap and trace the other side of the pedestal cut-out, as shown above.

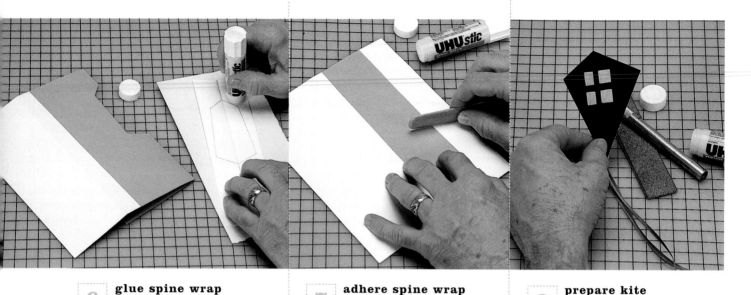

6 | **glue spine wrap**
Remove the spine wrap and apply glue to the areas outside the traced pedestal.

7 | **adhere spine wrap**
Adhere the spine wrap to the center fold of the card and burnish.

8 | **prepare kite**
Place the decorative paper for the kite face-up with the grain running vertically. Trace the kite pattern to the paper and cut it out. Fold the kite in half vertically, crease the fold and add a tail if desired.

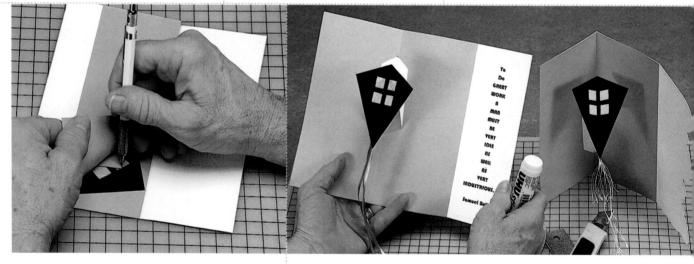

9 | **attach kite to pedestal**
Close the card, leaving the flap on the right side open. Lift the bottom right corner of the card and place the folded kite in the fold of the pedestal. Slide the kite back and forth until it is hidden when the card is closed. Lift the corner again and trace the pedestal point to the side of the kite. Remove the kite, open the card and apply glue to the pedestal. Close the card, lift the bottom right corner and attach the kite to the pedestal, using the traced line for placement. Close the card and burnish.

10 | **add text**
To finish, open the card to reveal the pedestal pop-up. Add text to the right flap and decorate the card as desired. The pedestal in the card on the left swings up from the bottom, and the pedestal in the card on the right swings down from the top.

TRYTHIS!

Combine the pop-up mechanisms in the Simple V Card and the Pedestal Card to make a new action card.

star dreams

The pedestal pattern was traced to this card after turning it around with the point facing down. This causes the star to swing up from the bottom instead of down like the kite in the step-by-step demo. The star pattern I used to make this card can be found on page 35.

>>

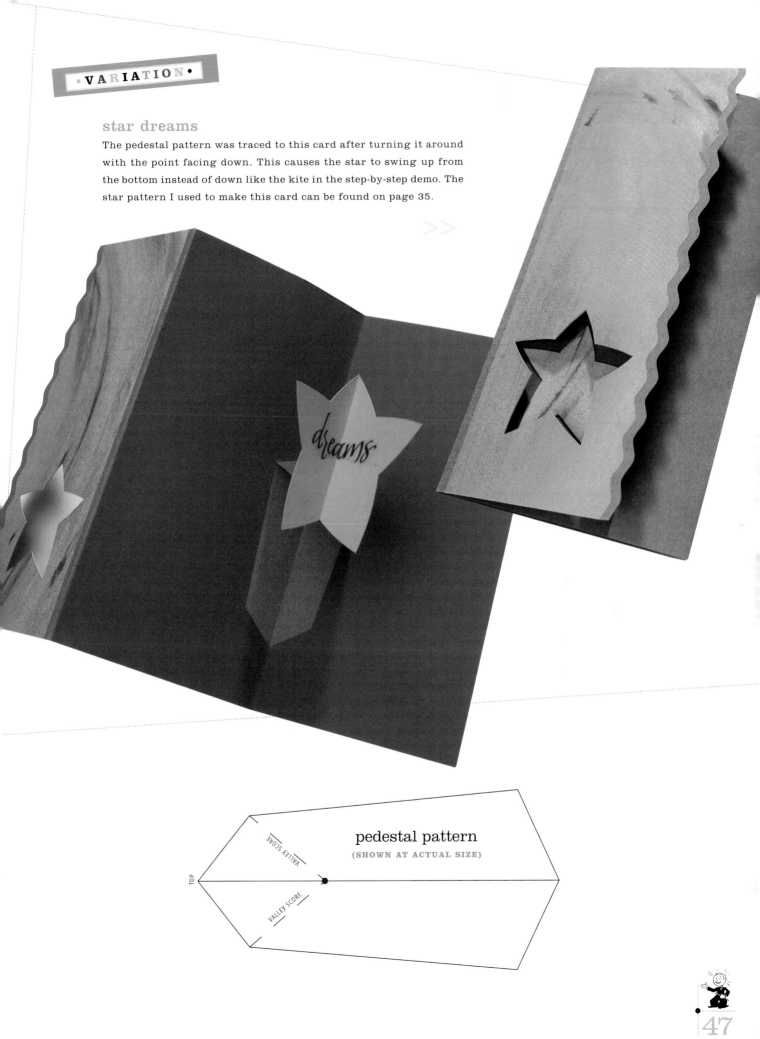

pedestal pattern
(SHOWN AT ACTUAL SIZE)

TOP

VALLEY SCORE

VALLEY SCORE

In 1998, I received a beautiful handmade Christmas card from artist Nichol Rauch. It had a wreath on the front made from cancelled postage stamps. With Nichol's permission, I designed a simple pop-up card featuring a similar postage stamp wreath. The Postal Wreath Card is the result. (Nichol also made the humorous Side-Pull V Card I'm holding in my hand on page 2.)

postal wreath
card

materials >>

card > a-2 card with full flap

wreath > 3" x 3" (7.6cm x 7.6cm) piece of cardstock

spine wrap > 2" x 5½" (5.1cm x 14cm) piece of decorative paper or cardstock (grain long)

scrap piece of mat board

wreath pattern (page 51)

ten to fifteen cancelled postage stamps

basic tool kit (page 8)

1 draw lines on card

Open the A-2 card and place it on your work surface with the flap pointing left. Measure down 1¼" (3.2cm) and 2½" (6.4cm) from the top and lightly draw horizontal lines, extending about 1" (2.5cm) to either side of the card's center fold. Then, lightly draw vertical lines ¾" (1.9cm) to the right and left of the center fold to connect the horizontal lines.

2 cut and score lines

Cut along the horizontal lines, starting and stopping at the vertical lines. Valley score the vertical lines. (For instructions, see pages 12–13.) Erase all remaining pencil lines. Push the cut and scored section to the inside of the card.

3 fold and crease right panel

Fold the right panel of the card to the left and crease the scores.

4 score, fold and crease spine wrap

Place the paper or cardstock for the spine wrap face-down on your work surface. Valley score, fold and crease it vertically down the center. Place the spine wrap flush against the center fold of the card, as shown above, and lay both components flat on your work surface.

5 adhere spine wrap

Open the spine wrap and trace the cut-out area of the card to the back of the spine wrap. Close the spine wrap and flip the card over to the right. Open the spine wrap again and trace the cut-out area to the other side of the spine wrap, as shown above. Remove the spine wrap from the card and apply glue outside the traced area, using glue guards. Adhere the spine wrap to the card's center fold and burnish.

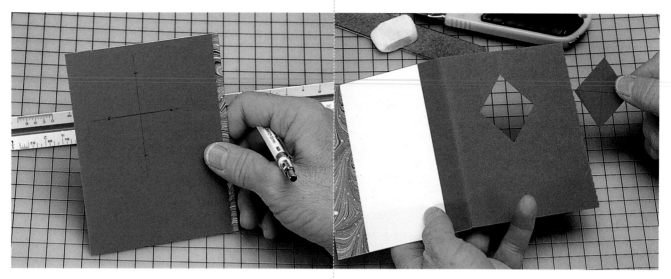

6 draw diamond shape

Close the flap and place the card on your work surface with the spine wrap pointing right. Measure over 1⅞" (4.8cm) from the flap fold and lightly draw a vertical line. Measure 1⅞" (4.8cm) down from the top and lightly draw a horizontal line. Make dots on the horizontal line ⅞" (2.2cm) to the left and right of the vertical line. Make dots on the vertical line 1⅛" (2.9cm) above and below the horizontal line. Connect the dots to form a diamond shape.

7 cut out diamond

Open the card and place it face-down with the flap pointing right. Cut out the diamond shape and erase all remaining pencil lines.

8 trace diamond to card

Close the card and lightly trace the diamond window to the front panel of the card. Open the flap and draw another diamond ⅛" (0.3cm) inside the first diamond.

9 cut out diamond

Place a scrap piece of mat board in the center of the card and cut out the inner diamond. Erase all remaining pencil lines and set the card aside.

10 transfer wreath pattern

Trace the wreath pattern to cardstock and cut it out.

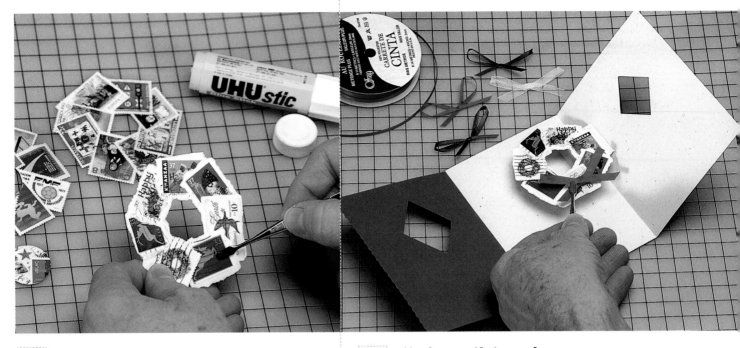

11 add stamps to wreath

Glue cancelled postage stamps to the wreath, keeping the maximum diameter of the wreath to 3¼" (8.3cm). Otherwise, the card won't close.

12 attach wreath to card

Glue the wreath to the right side of the pop-up mechanism on the inside of the card. Tie a small bow and glue it to the front of the wreath, using tweezers for precise placement.

13 embellish card

To finish, glue computer-generated text or words and images cut from old greeting cards to the card. Burnish.

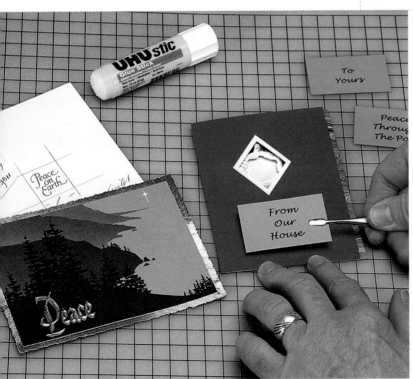

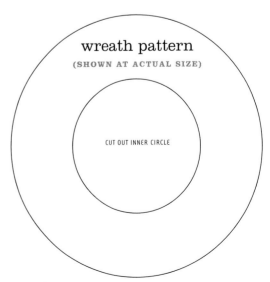

wreath pattern

(SHOWN AT ACTUAL SIZE)

CUT OUT INNER CIRCLE

The Stand-Up Card opens 180°, employs a striking use of positive and negative space and is easy to construct! A tree is featured in the step-by-step instructions, but once you understand how this card works, you can make almost any image "stand up." Use the star patterns on page 55 to make the stand-up star card pictured below, or use photos, drawn or stamped images or pictures from magazines to create your own.

stand-up
card

materials >>

card> a-2 card
with partial flap

tree > 3" x 3" (7.6cm x 7.6cm)
piece of decorative paper

liner > 3¼" x 4" (8.3cm x
10.2cm) piece of plain or
decorative paper

scrap piece of mat board

tree pattern (page 55)

liner pattern (page 55)

basic tool kit (page 8)

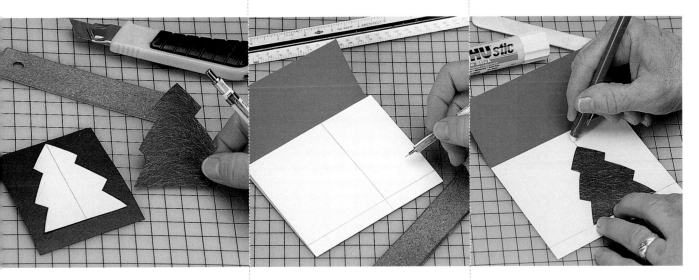

1 **cut out tree**
Trace the tree pattern to the 3" x 3" (7.6cm x 7.6cm) decorative paper and cut it out.

2 **prepare card**
Position the folded A-2 card with the flap open at the top. Measure over 3¼" (8.3cm) from the left edge and lightly draw a vertical line across the front panel. Measure up ½" (1.3cm) from the bottom and lightly draw a horizontal line.

3 **attach tree**
Glue the tree from step 1 to the front panel of the card, with the point at the top of the tree touching the vertical line and the bottom of the tree touching the horizontal line. Burnish and erase all remaining pencil lines.

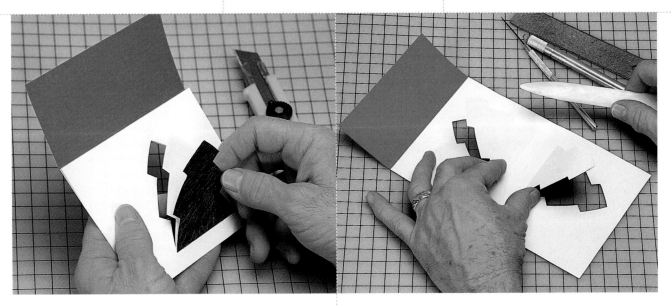

4 **cut around tree**
Use a utility knife to trim around each side of the tree, cutting through both layers of the card. Do not cut along the bottom of the tree.

5 **score, fold and crease trees**
Pierce two holes at the bottom of the tree where the sides meet the horizontal line. Open the card and valley score the bottom of each tree using the pierced holes to line up your ruler. Fold each tree along the score and crease. (For instructions, see pages 12–13.)

6 trace tree to flap

Close the card with the flap on top of both trees and under the front of the card, as shown above. Then, trace the top of the tree window to the flap.

7 cut out treetop

Open the card completely flat and cut out the traced treetop from the flap. Set the treetop aside for use in step 12.

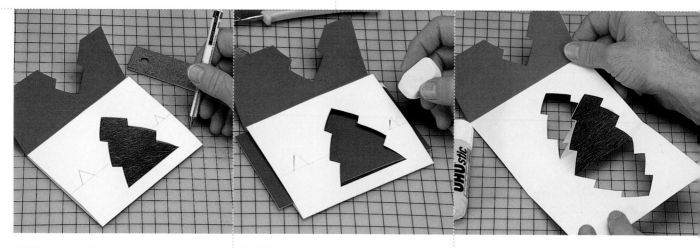

8 trace flap to front

Close the card and lightly trace the bottom left and right edges of the flap to the front of the card. Open the flap and draw two small inverted V shapes on the line on each side of the tree.

9 cut out inverted v

Place a scrap of mat board under the front panel of the card and cut down the sides of the inverted V shapes. The flap will tuck behind these slits to keep the card closed. Erase all remaining pencil lines.

10 glue treetops together

Open the card and glue the treetops together. Close the card and burnish.

11 add message

Trace the liner pattern to the liner paper and write, print or stamp a message inside the tracing. Cut out the liner and glue it to the inside of the card on the left side of the tree. Burnish.

12 add more trees

To finish the card, glue the small tree cut-out from step 7 to the bottom of the three-dimensional tree. Cut out small triangles from scraps of paper and glue them over the inverted V cuts on the front of the card. Decorate the front flap as desired.

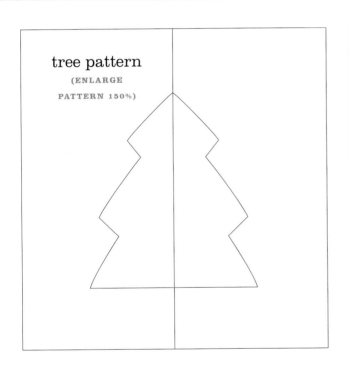

tree pattern
(ENLARGE PATTERN 150%)

liner pattern
(ENLARGE PATTERN 150%)

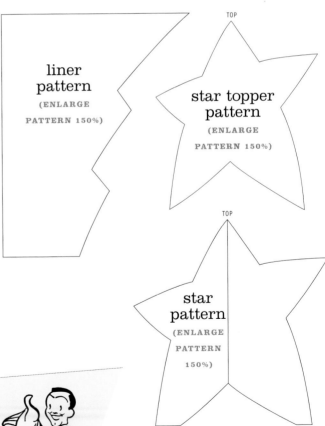

star topper pattern
(ENLARGE PATTERN 150%)

TOP

TOP

star pattern
(ENLARGE PATTERN 150%)

HELPFUL**HINT**

When making multiple Stand-Up Cards, trace the inside liner pattern several times to 8½" x 11" (21.6cm x 27.9cm) white paper. Add text inside each tracing, photocopy to decorative paper and cut the inside liners out as you need them.

The stylized tree that pops up in this card is an excellent example of the V-fold. It is literally an upside-down V. Other images will work with this card if the scores on either side of the vertical center fold create equal angles. The A-2 triptych tree pattern on page 59 works with both size cards.

triptych
card

materials >>

card > basic #10 card

tree > 7" x 7" (17.8cm x
17.8cm) piece of cardstock

liners > 3¹⁄₄" x 8¹⁄₄" (8.3cm x
21cm) piece of decorative
paper or cardstock
(grain long)

#10 triptych tree pattern
(page 59)

curve pattern (page 59)

basic tool kit (page 8)

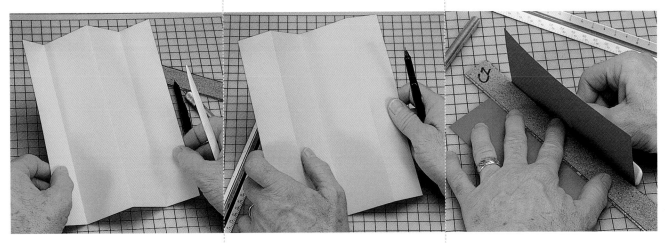

1 **score, fold and crease card**

Open the #10 card and place the inside surface face-down with the fold running vertically. Measure over 1⅝" (4.1cm) and 6⅜" (16.2cm) from the left edge and make tick marks near the top and bottom. Using the marks to align your ruler, make vertical valley scores, fold and crease. (For instructions, see pages 12–13.)

2 **make dot on card**

Flip the card over and make a dot on the center fold 2⅜" (6cm) from the top. Set the card aside for use in step 7.

3 **score, fold and crease tree cardstock**

Place the cardstock for the tree face-down with the grain running vertically. (For more about grain direction, see page 10.) Measure over 3½" (8.9cm) from the left edge and valley score vertically down the center. Fold and crease.

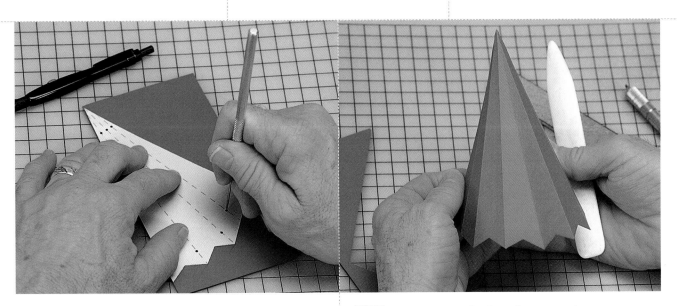

4 **transfer tree pattern**

Align the long edge of the #10 triptych tree pattern on the center fold of the tree cardstock with the point at the top. Trace the pattern and pierce holes through the six dots on the pattern.

5 **cut, score, fold and crease tree**

Remove the pattern and cut out the tree. Valley score six vertical lines on the inside surface of the tree cardstock, using the pierced holes for ruler placement. Fold the tree at each score and crease heavily, working left to right. Flip the tree over and fold again. If any folds still offer resistance, crease a second time. You now have a triptych tree, as shown above.

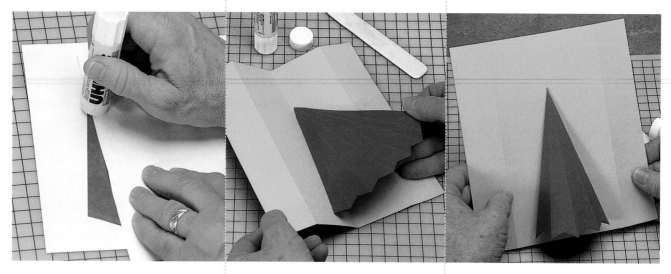

6 **apply glue to tree**
Fold the triptych tree in half and place it in the vertical position with the fold facing right. Apply glue to the wedge-shaped panel on the left, using a glue guard to cover the rest of the panels.

7 **adhere left side of tree**
Place the fold of the triptych tree against the center fold of the card with the top of the tree touching the dot you drew in step 2. Close the card and burnish. Allow the glue to dry for about one minute, then reopen the card.

8 **adhere right side of tree**
With the triptych tree still folded, apply glue to the wedge-shaped panel on the right, using a glue guard to cover the rest of the panels. Close the card and burnish. Allow the glue to dry, then reopen the card to reveal the triptych tree.

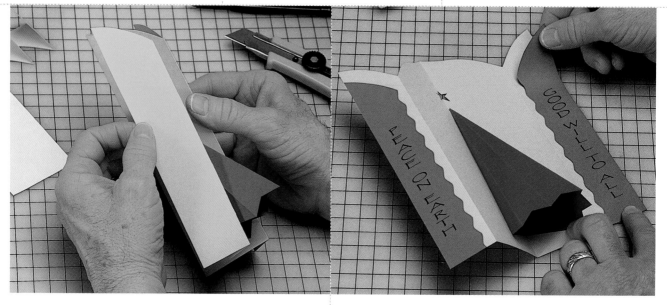

9 **add curves**
Close the card and fold back the outer panels. Place the long edge of the curve pattern on the center fold of the card with the point of the pattern at the top. Trace the curve. Use the utility knife to cut along the curved line through all the layers of the card, making several passes if necessary.

10 **add embellishments**
To finish the card, cut liners from decorative paper or cardstock and glue them in place. Add a message and decorate as desired.

greetings

The A-2 triptych tree pattern below creates a smaller tree that works equally well in A-2 cards (shown here) and #10 cards. The text band can be glued to the left and right panels at any angle. Use the curve pattern below to shape the top of your card, or create a unique curve of your own.

GREETINGS of the SEASON

curve
pattern
(ENLARGE
PATTERN 135%)

PLACE THIS EDGE ON CENTER FOLD

PLACE THIS EDGE ON CENTER FOLD

a-2 triptych tree pattern
(ENLARGE PATTERN 135%)

#10 triptych tree pattern
(ENLARGE PATTERN 135%)

PLACE THIS EDGE ON CENTER FOLD

Triangle Cards can be elegant and sophisticated, or whimsical and funky, depending on the papers you choose. Four hinged triangle flaps hide and reveal text and create ever-changing patterns as they are raised and lowered. This project starts with a basic #10 card. However, you can easily change the size of the components to work with an A-2 card. Or, add another triangle fold-over inside the full flap on a #10 card for even more surprises! So many possibilities, so little time.

triangle
card

materials >>

card > basic #10 card

inside liners > two 3½ x 7"
(8.9cm x 17.8cm) pieces of
plain paper (grain long)

triangle fold-overs > two
3½" x 7" (8.9cm x 17.8cm)
pieces of decorative paper
(grain long)

triangle liners > two 3⅛" x
3⅛" (7.9cm x 7.9cm) pieces
of decorative paper

liner for front of card >
8" x 3½" (20.3cm x 8.9cm)
piece of decorative paper
(grain long)

basic tool kit (page 8)

1 attach inside liners

Open the basic #10 card and place it on your work surface with the inside face-up. Glue the inside liners to each side of the card, centered top to bottom and about ⅛" (0.3cm) from the center fold. Burnish.

2 make triangle fold-overs

Place one of the triangle fold-overs face-down on your work surface. Fold the top and bottom left corners to the right edge to form a triangle. Crease the folds. Repeat with the other fold-over, folding the corners to the left edge. Flip the triangles over and apply glue to the back surfaces. Attach the triangles to the liners, pointing outward as shown. Unfold the four small corner triangles and burnish.

TRYTHIS!

For a completely different effect, glue the triangle fold-overs to the inside of the card pointing inward.

3 cut and attach triangle liners

Cut the triangle liner pieces in half diagonally. Glue the liners to the inside surfaces of the triangle fold-overs. Burnish.

TRYTHIS!

Make a #10 envelope out of matching decorative paper. (For instructions, see page 29.)

4 add front liner

Fold in all the triangles and close the card. Glue the front liner to the front panel and burnish.

Slider Cards consist of two basic components: a sleeve and a slider. Deceptively thin, they are easy to make and can be oriented so the slider opens up, down or to either side. With a little planning, you can make cards with sliders on both sides! This project shows you how to make an A-2 Slider Card and a #10 Slider Card. The basic steps are the same—only the measurements and cardstock sizes differ.

slider
card

THE MORE YOU USE IT,
THE MORE YOU HAVE...

MAYA ANGELOU

<< materials

a-2 slider card

card > 9" x 5½" (22.9cm x 14cm) piece of cardstock (grain short)

slider > 4½" x 4" (11.4cm x 10.2cm) piece of cardstock (grain long)

basic tool kit (page 8)

#10 slider card

card > 9" x 8½" (22.9cm x 21.6cm) piece of cardstock (grain short)

slider > 6⅞" x 3⅝" (17.5cm x 9.2cm) piece of cardstock (grain long)

basic tool kit (page 8)

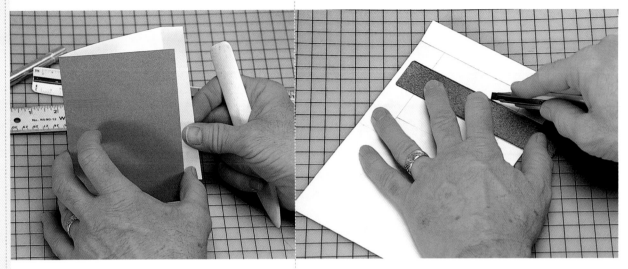

1 **score, fold and crease card**

Place the A-2 cardstock face-down in the horizontal position. Measure over 4" (10.2cm) and 8⅛" (20.6cm) from the left edge and make two vertical valley scores. Fold and crease each score. (For instructions, see pages 12–13.)

2 **draw and cut lines**

Position the card with the narrow panel pointing right. Measure down 1" (2.5cm) and 4½" (11.4cm) from the top edge of the middle panel and draw two horizontal lines. Then, draw two vertical lines across the middle panel ⅞" (2.2cm) and 3¼" (8.3cm) to the right of the left fold. Cut along the vertical lines, starting and stopping at the horizontal lines.

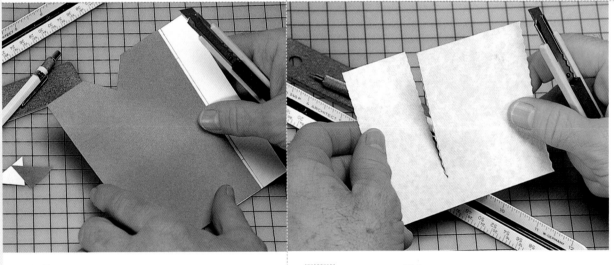

3 **cut notch in card**

Fold the left panel over the middle panel. Cut a notch ¾" (1.9cm) deep and 1" (2.5cm) wide through the top center of both panels, as shown. Set the card aside.

4 **prepare slider**

Place the A-2 slider cardstock face-down in the horizontal position. Measure over 1¾" (4.4cm) from the left edge and draw a vertical line. Make a dot on the line 3¼" (8.3cm) down from the top and cut along the vertical line to the dot.

5 assemble card

Open the card from step 3 and place it face-down with the narrow panel pointing right. Hold the slider horizontally with the open end of the slit pointing toward the left. Slide the bottom section of the slider through the vertical slits in the card. The top section will be fully visible. Fold the left panel to the right, apply glue to the narrow panel and fold it to the left, over the right panel. Burnish.

6 add message

Flip the card over so that the slider pulls out to the right. With the slider closed, add the first part of your message to the right side of the card. Pull the slider open and add the second part of your message to the left side of the card.

1 fold, crease and score card

Place the cardstock for the #10 Slider Card face-down in the horizontal position. Measure over 3¾" (9.5cm) and 7⅝" (19.4cm) from the left edge and make vertical valley scores. Fold and crease each score.

2 prepare card and slider

Follow step 2 from the a-2 Slider Card, with the horizontal lines measuring 1½" (3.8cm) and 7" (17.8cm) down from the top edge and the vertical lines measuring 1" (2.5cm) and 2⅞" (7.3cm) to the right of the left fold. Cut the vertical lines, then fold and notch as you did in step 3. For the slider, draw the vertical line 2¾" (7cm) from the left edge and the dot 2⅞" (7.3cm) down from the top. Cut along the line to the dot.

3 assemble card and add message

Assemble the card and slider as you did in step 5 for the A-2 Slider Card. Close the card to determine the location and size of the text areas. Remove the slider and add text to the card, or glue a piece of paper with text onto the card. Insert the slider, glue the narrow panel to the card and burnish.

creativity

The horizontal slits on your slider cards can be cut at angles to create a wedge-shaped panel for your text. Consider adding text to the exposed section of the slider when it is pulled all the way out, or add decorative paper to the outer edge of the slider.

You can't use up CrEAtiviTY.

The more you use it, the more you have...
Maya Angelou

· VARIATIONS ·

Per ardua ad astra

reach for the stars

I covered the cardstock slider on this card with beautiful paper hand-painted by Rae K Du SSollae. The text was printed on colored paper, then trimmed and glued to the card. I stamped the stars with my own hand-carved image. The wavy edges on the slider add visual interest.

(By striving we reach the stars)

Congratulations on achieving your MFA!! Let's do dinner (on me) to celebrate!

Pull the sides of this one-piece Swivel Card and watch the center panel revolve 180°! The message swivels back and forth as the card is opened and closed. Stand the Swivel Card upright and it becomes a beautiful mini sculpture, offering a captivating view from either side. The step-by-step instructions demonstrate how to make a basic card with a rectangular center panel, like the one shown below, and a card with a leaf-shaped panel.

swivel
card

materials >>

card > 7¼" x 5½" (18.4cm x 14cm) piece of cardstock (grain short)

leaf > 5" x 5" (12.7cm x 12.7cm) piece of decorative paper

scrap of plain or decorative paper (for message)

leaf pattern (page 69)

basic tool kit (page 8)

One must still have chaos in oneself...

1 draw lines and dots

Place the cardstock for the card face-down in the horizontal position. Measure over 2⅞" (7.3cm) and 4⅜" (11.1cm) from the left edge and lightly draw two vertical lines from top to bottom. Then, measure down 1" (2.5cm) and 4" (10.2cm) from the top and draw two horizontal lines from side to side. Make dots on the right vertical line at the top and bottom, and at the point where the horizontal line intersects, as shown in the photo.

2 draw more lines

Draw two more vertical lines 1¾" (4.4cm) and 5½" (14cm) from the left edge, starting and stopping at the top and bottom horizontal lines.

3 cut around rectangles

Cut around the top, left and bottom of the left rectangle. Then, cut around the top, right and bottom of the right rectangle.

4 score, fold and crease card

Valley score the upper and lower parts of the left vertical line, fold and crease the scores. (For instructions, see pages 12–13.) Open the card and pierce holes through the four dots you drew in step 1. Flip the card over and mountain score the upper and lower parts of the right vertical line, using the pierced holes to align your ruler. Fold and crease the scores and erase all remaining pencil lines.

5   add message to small panel

Push the sides of the card together to close it. Position it face-up with the small panel toward the right. Write or print the first part of your message on a paper rectangle slightly smaller than the panel (or write directly on the panel), cut it out and glue it in place, using tweezers for precise placement. Burnish.

6   add message to large panel

Pull the sides of the card apart to open it. Write, print or stamp the second part of your message on a paper rectangle slightly smaller than the large panel, cut it out and glue it in place.

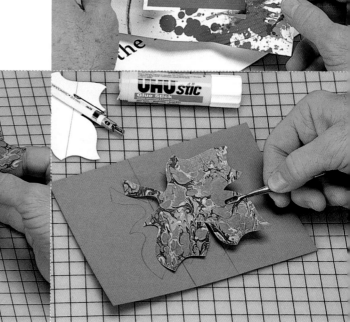

leaf swivel card

1   transfer pattern

Position the lines on the leaf pattern running parallel with the grain direction of the decorative paper. (For more about grain direction, see page 10.) Trace and cut out the pattern.

TRY THIS!

Make Swivel Cards with the fish and heart patterns on page 69 as well. For a heart Swivel Card, align the single vertical line on the pattern with the left line on the card, centered top to bottom, and trace. Glue the heart to the card and cut around the left half of the heart. Valley score, fold and crease the upper and lower part of the vertical line. Mountain score the right vertical line along the entire length. Fold and crease.

2   add shape to card

Place the cardstock for the card in the horizontal position and measure over 2⅞" (7.3cm) and 4⅜" (11.1cm) from the left edge. Lightly draw two vertical lines from top to bottom. Center the leaf pattern on the cardstock, aligning the vertical lines on the pattern with the vertical lines you just drew. Trace the pattern onto the cardstock. Apply glue to the back of the leaf from step 1 and glue it in place, using the tracing for placement and tweezers for proper alignment. Burnish. Erase all remaining pencil lines.

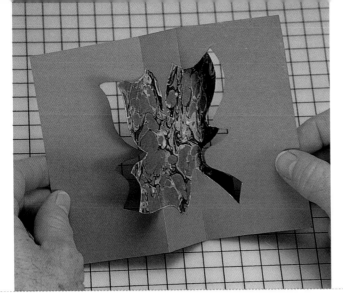

score, fold and crease card

Cut around each side of the leaf, starting and stopping at the vertical lines on the card. Valley score the left vertical line and mountain score the right vertical line above and below the edges of the leaf. Fold and crease the scores. The card may be oriented with the stem at the top or bottom.

TRYTHIS!

Flip the leaf pattern over and trace a mirror image onto another piece of paper. Cut it out and glue it onto the back of the other leaf.

happy holidays

Almost any image can be used for a swivel card. Narrow shapes, like this tree or the heart below, are cut only around the left side of the image. When the card is opened, the image flips to the back, leaving the middle section of the card intact and creating more surface area for text or imagery.

>>

HAPPY HOLIDAYS

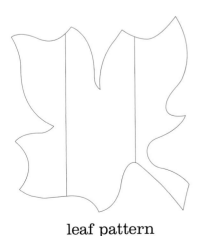

leaf pattern
(ENLARGE PATTERN 200%)

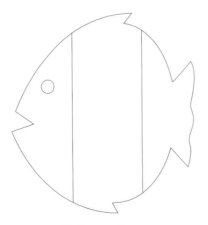

fish pattern
(ENLARGE PATTERN 200%)

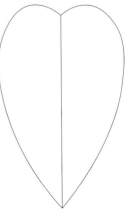

heart pattern
(ENLARGE PATTERN 200%)

Spiral Cards are fun to make and operate. It is impressive to see a flat circle blossom into a three-dimensional spiral. The A-2 cards shown below, which have one spiral each, are quick and easy to make. The #10 Ho-Ho-Ho Card on page 73 heightens the surprise element by incorporating three spirals. For a completely different look, try making cards with one spiral and additional windows for text and illustrations.

spiral
card

materials >>

card > a-2 card with full flap

window pattern>
4¹⁄₈" x 5½" (10.5cm x 14cm)
scrap piece of cardstock

spiral > 3½" x 3½"
(8.9cm x 8.9cm) piece
of decorative paper

alphabet stickers or
large alphabet stamps

circle template, compass
or circle cutter

craft glue

basic tool kit (page 8)

1 prepare window pattern

Place the window pattern cardstock in the vertical position. Measure over 2⅛" (5.4cm) from the left edge and draw a vertical line from top to bottom. Measure down 2¾" (7cm) from the top and draw a horizontal line from side to side. Make an X in the upper-left corner of the cardstock to indicate the top of your pattern.

2 make diamond window

Measure 1" (2.5cm) up and down from the horizontal line and make dots on the vertical line. Measure ¾" (1.9cm) to the left and right of the vertical line and make dots on the horizontal line. Line your ruler up on the dots and cut out the diamond-shaped window.

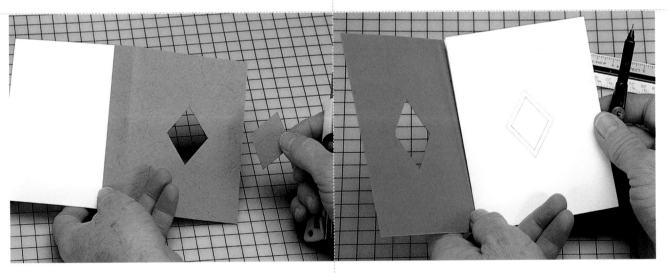

3 cut out flap window

Open the A-2 card and place it face-down on your work surface with the flap pointing right. Place the window pattern (with the X at the top) directly over the flap, trace the diamond shape and cut it out.

4 cut out card window

Close the flap and trace the diamond shape to the front panel of the card. Open the flap and draw a smaller diamond ⅛" (0.3cm) inside the first diamond. Cut out the inner shape and erase all remaining pencil lines.

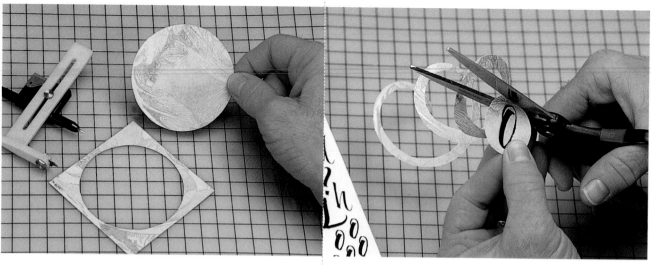

5 cut out circle
Use a circle cutter, compass or template to cut a 3" (7.6cm) circle from your spiral paper.

6 prepare spiral
Peel the middle letter of your word from the alphabet sticker sheet and adhere it to the center of the circle. Burnish. Cut the circle into a spiral, starting at the outside edge and working your way inward until you reach the letter.

TRYTHIS!

If you prefer, use alphabet rubber stamps instead of stickers.

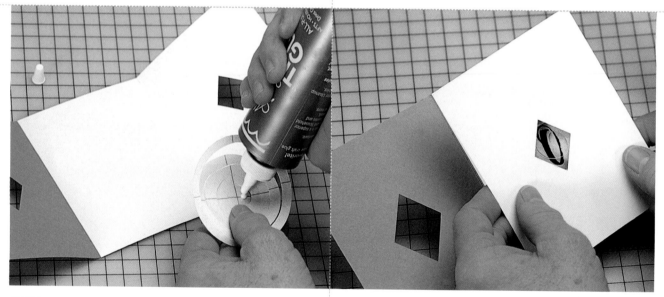

7 attach center of spiral to card
Flip the spiral over and squeeze a tiny dab of craft glue onto the center. The craft glue is more durable for this card and will hold the spiral in place. Attach the spiral to the center of the card's inside panel.

8 check for placement
Close the card to make sure the letter is centered in the window. Burnish the center of the spiral.

9 attach end of spiral to flap

Open the card completely and apply a thin coat of craft glue over the outer 1½" (3.8cm) of the spiral. Gently flatten out the spiral. Close the card and hold for a few seconds while the glue dries, so that you glue the end of the spiral to the inside flap.

10 add remaining letters

To finish, add the remaining letter stickers to the front of the card. Burnish.

• VARIATION •

ho-ho-ho

A-2 and #10 Spiral Cards are faster and easier to make when they don't have flaps, since windows only need to be cut on the front of the card. I hand-carved the letter and star stamps on the card above. Barbara Richards created the playful text—Greetings of the Season—on her computer.

The Shaker Card is made from foam core and resembles a wrapped present when sent through the mail. Window openings can be any shape and hold a wide variety of objects, making it easy to tailor your card to a specific hobby, occupation or event. This card also doubles as a keepsake gift, and it arrives in its own wrapper made from decorative paper.

shaker
card

materials >>

card > 4¼" x 5½" (10.8cm x 14cm) piece of foam core

window > 4¼" x 5½" (10.8cm x 14cm) piece of 4mm or 5mm polyester film

liners (front and back) > two 4¼" x 5½" (10.8cm x 14cm) pieces of cardstock (grain long)

wrapper > 9¾" x 8½" (24.8cm x 21.6cm) piece of decorative paper

closure sticker > 3" x 3" (7.6cm x 7.6cm) piece of decorative paper

patterns > two 4¼" x 5½" (10.8cm x 14cm) pieces of cardstock

black marker

findings and tiny objects (for window)

basic tool kit (page 8)

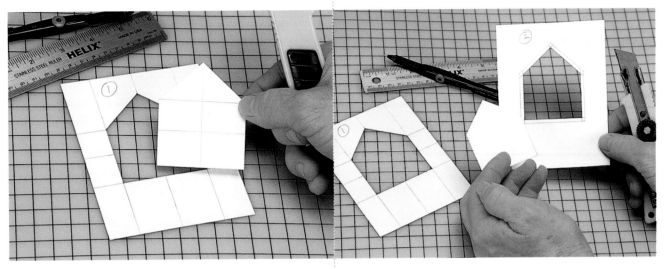

1 create pattern 1

Write the number "1" in the upper-left corner of a piece of scrap cardstock to indicate that it is pattern 1. Cut out a window in your desired shape and set the cut-out piece aside.

2 create pattern 2

Place pattern 1 over another piece of scrap cardstock and trace window opening. Measure in $1/8"$ (0.3cm) from the tracing and draw the shape again. Cut out the inner shape and set the cut-out piece aside. Write the number "2" in the upper-left corner to indicate that this is pattern 2.

3 prepare foam core

Trace pattern 1 to the foam core and cut out the window. Color the foam core edges inside the window and around the perimeter with a black marker.

4 attach back liner

Apply glue to one side of the foam core and adhere it to the inside surface of one of the cardstock liners. Burnish the liner.

5 prepare front liner

Trace pattern 2 to the top surface of the remaining cardstock liner. Cut out the window shape and save it for step 6.

6 fill window

Place the cut-out window shape from step 5 inside the foam core window and glue it down if desired. Place tiny objects, stamped or written words or phrases, pieces of paper, beads and other findings inside the window opening, making sure the pieces you select are thinner than the foam core.

7 add polyester film

Apply glue to the top surface of the foam core, right up to the edges of the window opening. Adhere the polyester film to the foam core and burnish.

8 attach front liner

Apply glue to the back surface of the remaining liner and attach it to the front of the card over the polyester film. Burnish.

9 position card on wrapper

Place the decorative paper wrapper face-down in the horizontal position. Position the Shaker Card in the center of the wrapper, skewed diagonally, as shown.

HELPFUL**HINT**

Acetate tears and scratches easily. Polyester film is crystal clear, dimensionally stable and resists tearing and scratching.

10 **wrap left and right corners**
Wrap the bottom-left corner snugly around the left side of the card and the upper-right corner around the right side of the card. Tape in place.

11 **tuck corners**
Tuck in all four corners of the decorative paper with your bone folder.

12 **wrap remaining corners**
To finish, wrap the two remaining corners snugly around the card and secure them with tape. Cut a shape out of decorative paper and glue it in place to conceal the tape. Cut or tear an address label from plain paper and glue it to the front of the card. Embellish as desired.

·VARIATION·

monkey shaker
Tiny transistors were used to create the "cage" for this asian-themed card. Notice how the decorative paper theme is maintained with phrases inside the window. A limited color palette creates visual drama as well.

>>

My design for the Signal Card is based on a World War II device used by the Navy to teach Morse code. Friend and architect Dick Peterson stopped by one evening to describe a wonderful paper object he had seen at a swap meet. He made a simple sketch, and my wheels started turning. I produced a rough model right there at the kitchen counter and started refining it the next day. The step-by-step instructions for this project demonstrate how to make one Signal Card, but with one small hinge piece and another Signal Card, you can replicate the double Signal Card pictured below.

signal
card

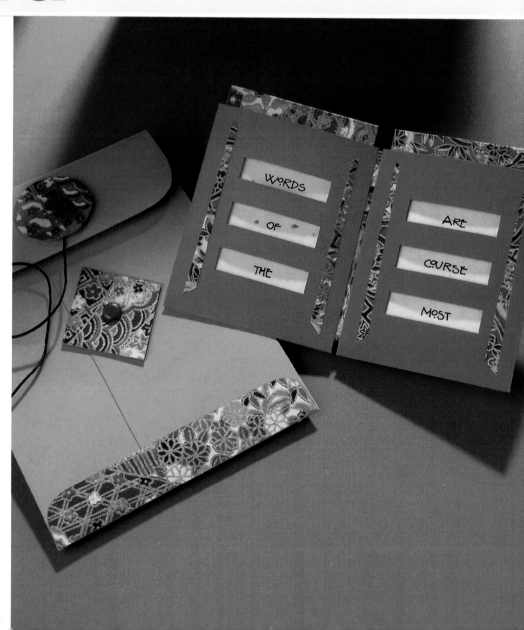

materials >>

signal card > 8½" x 11" (21.6cm x 27.9cm) piece of cardstock (grain short)

stiffener > 2⅝" x 3⅝" (6.7cm x 9.2cm) piece of cardstock (grain long)

hinge (optional) > 2" x 2⅞" (5.1cm x 7.3cm) piece of cardstock (grain long)

plain or decorative paper (for message, optional)

signal card pattern (page 81)

basic tool kit (page 8)

1 **transfer pattern**

Trace the Signal Card pattern to the cardstock for the Signal Card. Pierce eight holes in the cardstock through the dots on the pattern.

2 **cut out card**

Cut out the Signal Card, including the windows. (For instructions, see page 14.)

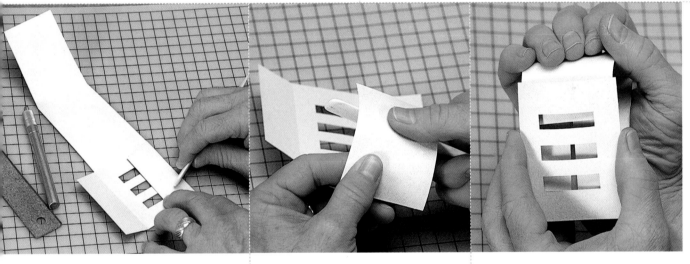

3 **score, fold and crease card**

Using the pierced holes to align your ruler, valley score the inside surface of the card as indicated by the lines on the pattern. Fold and crease. (For instructions, see pages 12–13.)

4 **curve top flap**

Run the inside surface of the top flap over your bone folder to create a slight curve. This makes it easier to tuck the flap behind the windows in the next step.

5 **tuck in top flap**

Fold the side flaps in toward the center, then fold the bottom flap with the windows up to make a pocket. Cup your hand around the curve on the top flap and gently guide it into the pocket.

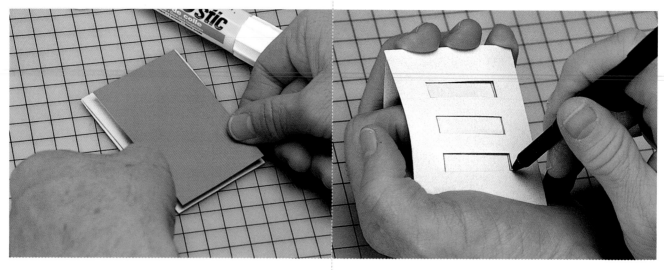

6 **add stiffener**

Place the card with the windows face-down. Apply glue to the back of the stiffener cardstock and attach it to the back of the card. Burnish.

7 **trace window openings**

Flip the card over and lightly trace the three window openings. Then, squeeze down on the top of the card as shown and trace the window openings again.

8 **number boxes**

Place the opened card on your work surface with the window openings at the top and the traced window boxes at the bottom, as shown above. Number the boxes from top to bottom in the following order: 4, 1, 5, 2, 6 and 3. Close the card as you did in step 5. Windows 1, 2 and 3 will be visible when the card is relaxed, and windows 4, 5 and 6 will appear when the card is squeezed.

TRYTHIS!

If desired, cut out and glue decorative paper or cardstock to the top flap before tracing the window openings. This will create a colorful area for your text.

9 **add message**

Write your text phrase directly inside the six window boxes in the correct sequence (4, 1, 5, 2, 6 and 3). The computer-generated text panel in my left hand above, when glued in place, reads, "Imagination is intelligence" in the relaxed position. When squeezed, the second half of the phrase, "having fun . . . Anonymous," is revealed. I added decorative triangle shapes above and below the windows on the front of the card as a design element.

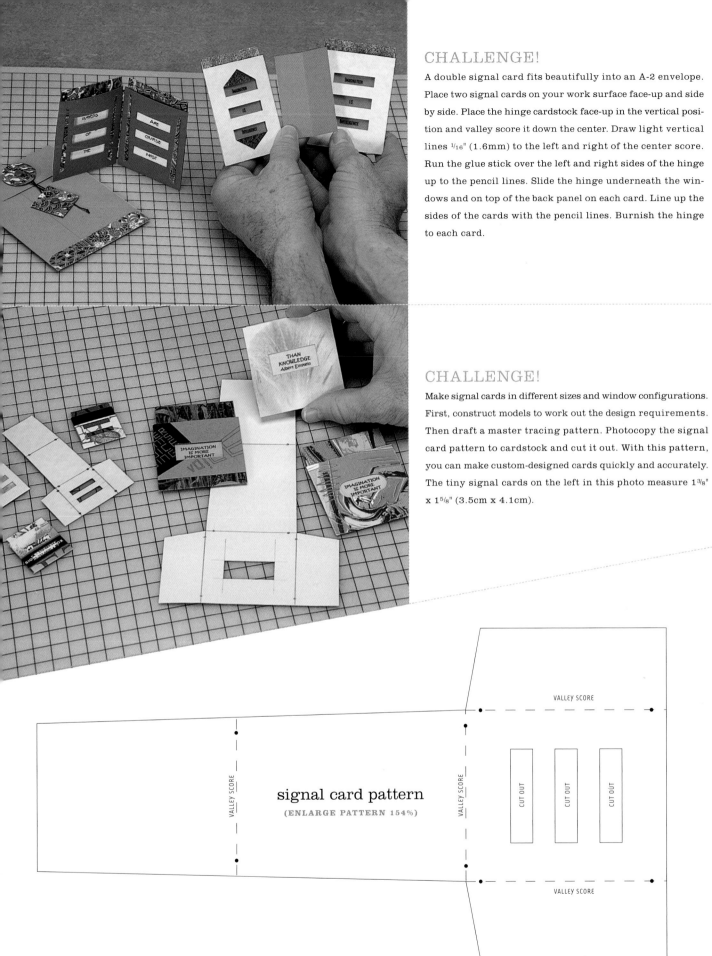

CHALLENGE!

A double signal card fits beautifully into an A-2 envelope. Place two signal cards on your work surface face-up and side by side. Place the hinge cardstock face-up in the vertical position and valley score it down the center. Draw light vertical lines 1/16" (1.6mm) to the left and right of the center score. Run the glue stick over the left and right sides of the hinge up to the pencil lines. Slide the hinge underneath the windows and on top of the back panel on each card. Line up the sides of the cards with the pencil lines. Burnish the hinge to each card.

CHALLENGE!

Make signal cards in different sizes and window configurations. First, construct models to work out the design requirements. Then draft a master tracing pattern. Photocopy the signal card pattern to cardstock and cut it out. With this pattern, you can make custom-designed cards quickly and accurately. The tiny signal cards on the left in this photo measure 1 3/8" x 1 5/8" (3.5cm x 4.1cm).

VALLEY SCORE

VALLEY SCORE

VALLEY SCORE

CUT OUT CUT OUT CUT OUT

signal card pattern
(ENLARGE PATTERN 154%)

VALLEY SCORE

This card is made from a single piece of cardstock with one window and four scores. Add text and send it as is, or glue it to a covered board, as pictured below, to frame it and give it more substance. Make a few Sliding Text Cards using the pattern provided, then design your own in larger and smaller sizes with two or more windows.

sliding text
card

materials >>

card > 8½" x 11" (21.6cm x 27.9cm) piece of cardstock (grain short)

liners > 8½" x 11" (21.6cm x 27.9cm) piece of decorative paper

sliding text card pattern (page 85)

covered a-2 or #10 board (optional)

basic tool kit (page 8)

1 **transfer pattern and cut out card**
   Place the cardstock for the card face-down in the horizontal position. Place the pattern along the bottom edge of the cardstock, squared up with the bottom left corner. Trace the pattern, including the window, and pierce holes in the cardstock through the eight dots on the pattern. Cut out the card, including the window.

2 **score, fold and crease card**
   Using the pierced holes to align your ruler, valley score the first, second and fourth lines, and mountain score the third line, as indicated on the pattern. Fold and crease all scores. (For instructions, see pages 12–13.)

3 **glue and burnish panels**
   Apply glue to the inside surface of panel three and adhere it to panel two. Burnish.

4 **trace window opening**
   Trace the window opening in panel four to panel three.

5 **cut out window**
   Cut out the traced window opening. You will be cutting through two layers of cardstock (panels two and three), so be sure to place your ruler cork-side down. (For instructions, see page 14.)

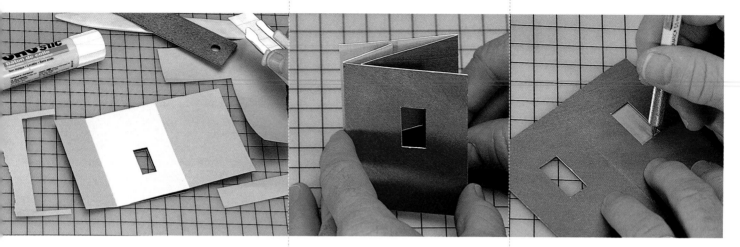

6 **line panels**

Open the card and place it face-down with the narrow panel pointing left. Glue the liner paper to panels one and five and trim away the excess paper.

7 **fold card**

Fold the narrow panel to the right and the large panel to the left. Flip the card over top to bottom so that the window is in the upper-right corner.

8 **trace window opening**

Keeping the card closed, place it flat on your work surface and lightly trace the window opening to the large panel underneath. Open the top flap and trace the window to the narrow panel.

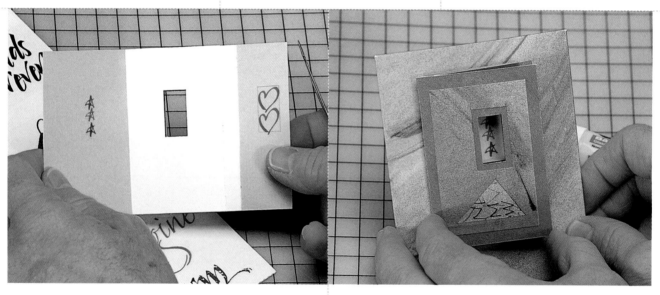

9 **add message**

Open the card and place text and/or illustrations in the traced window areas. Erase all remaining pencil lines. The text on the larger panel will be visible when the card is closed, and the text on the smaller panel will slide into the window when the card is opened.

TRYTHIS!

Before placing your text, play around with the card. It can open to the top, bottom or either side. Text can be placed to read vertically or horizontally.

10 **decorate front of card**

Decorate the front of the card as desired. Send it as is, or apply glue to the back of the card and attach it to a covered A-2 (shown above) or #10 board.

two on one

Sliding text cards can be combined on the
front or back of a covered #10 mat board.
Or, mount one or two units on the front
of a #10 card, and one or two additional units inside the card. There
are so many possibilities.

>>

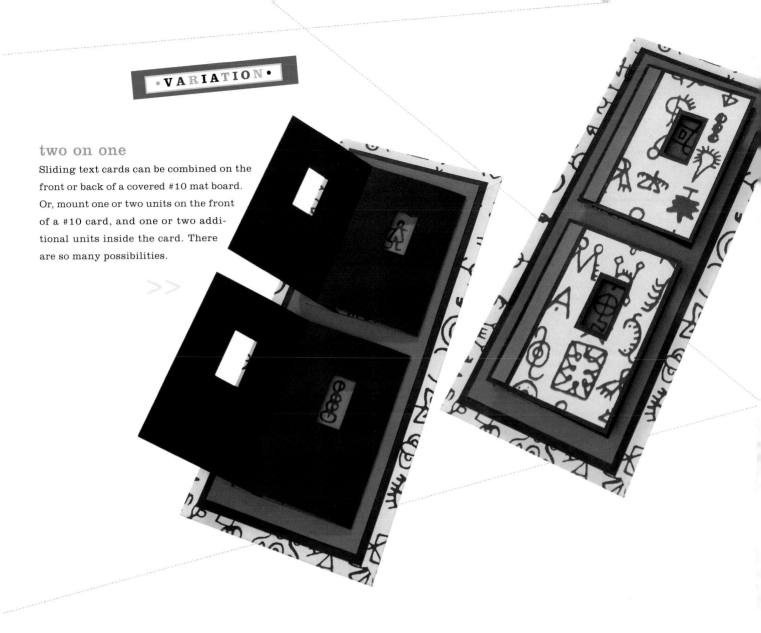

sliding text
pattern

(ENLARGE

PATTERN 143%)

VALLEY SCORE

VALLEY SCORE

MOUNTAIN SCORE

CUT OUT

VALLEY SCORE

A sleeve, a slider and five pages are assembled in a straightforward manner to produce the delightfully interactive Flip Card. The pages flip smoothly back and forth when a paper tab is pulled and pushed. Fold in the pull-tab and send your flip card in an A-2 envelope, or mount it to a #10 card or covered board and send it in a #10 envelope.

flip
card

materials >>

slider > 2³/₄" x 11" (7cm x 27.9cm) piece of cardstock (grain short)

sleeve > 8" x 2½" (20.3cm x 6.4cm) piece of cardstock (grain short)

pages > five 3¼" x 2½" (8.3cm x 6.4cm) pieces of cardstock (grain long)

basic #10 card or covered #10 board (optional)

basic tool kit (page 8)

1 draw lines

Place the slider cardstock face-down in the vertical position. Measure down from the top and draw horizontal lines at 3¼" (8.3cm), 3⅝" (9.2cm), 4" (10.2cm), 4⅜" (11.1cm), 4¾" (12.1cm), 5⅛" (13cm) and 10⅜" (26.4cm).

2 score, fold and crease

Valley score, fold and crease each line. (For instructions, see pages 12–13.) Then, crease all but the bottom score a second time to "soften" the folds. This prevents the pages from sticking together as they flip.

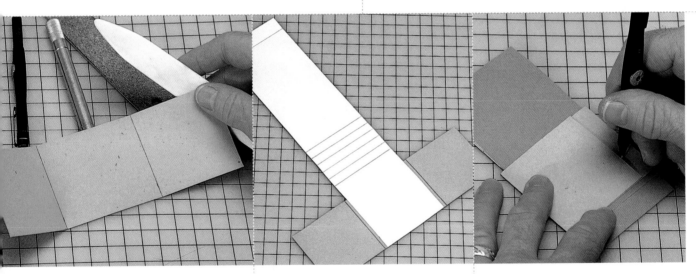

3 prepare sleeve

Place the sleeve cardstock face-down in the horizontal position. Measure over from the left edge and draw vertical lines at 2½" (6.4cm) and 5½" (14cm). Valley score, fold and crease both lines.

4 glue sleeve to slider

Apply glue to the center section of the sleeve on the valley fold side, keeping the glue approximately ⅛" (0.3cm) away from each fold. Hold the slider valley fold side up with the small panel at the top and attach the bottom section to the sleeve flush with the bottom and centered between the folds. Burnish.

5 fold and trace sleeve flap

Fold down the slider at the score nearest the center. Fold in the right flap on the sleeve, then the left flap. Trace the edge of the left flap to the right flap.

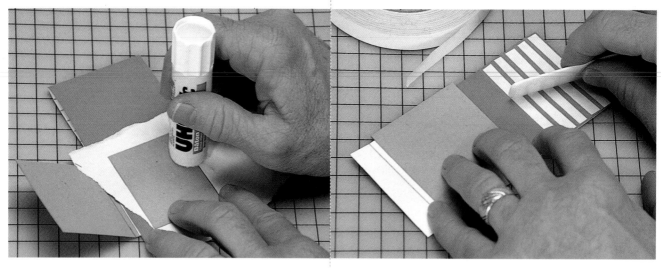

6   glue side flap

Lift the left side flap, place a glue guard under the right side flap and along the traced line, and apply glue to the right flap. Remove the glue guard, close the left flap and burnish.

7   apply tape to sections

Flip the slider/sleeve component over with the scores face-up. Place a strip of double-sided tape about ¼" (0.6cm) wide and 2½" (6.4cm) long on each of the five sections, centered side to side and top to bottom. Lightly burnish the top surface of each tape strip.

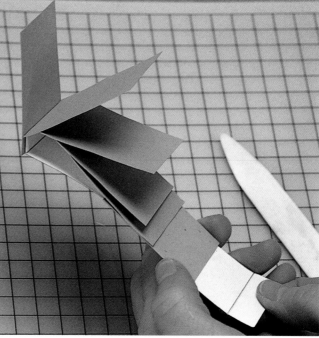

8   add pages

Remove the backing from the bottom tape strip. Place the long edge of a cardstock page along the fold above the tape strip, centered side to side. Burnish. Tape the four additional pages in place, working from bottom to top, keeping the sides aligned with the sides on the bottom page. Burnish each page as it is taped in place.

9   test slider action

Hold the card at the sides of the sleeve and gently pull and push the slider back and forth to test it.

HELPFUL**HINT**

Use the tip of your craft knife if the backing on the tape is difficult to remove.

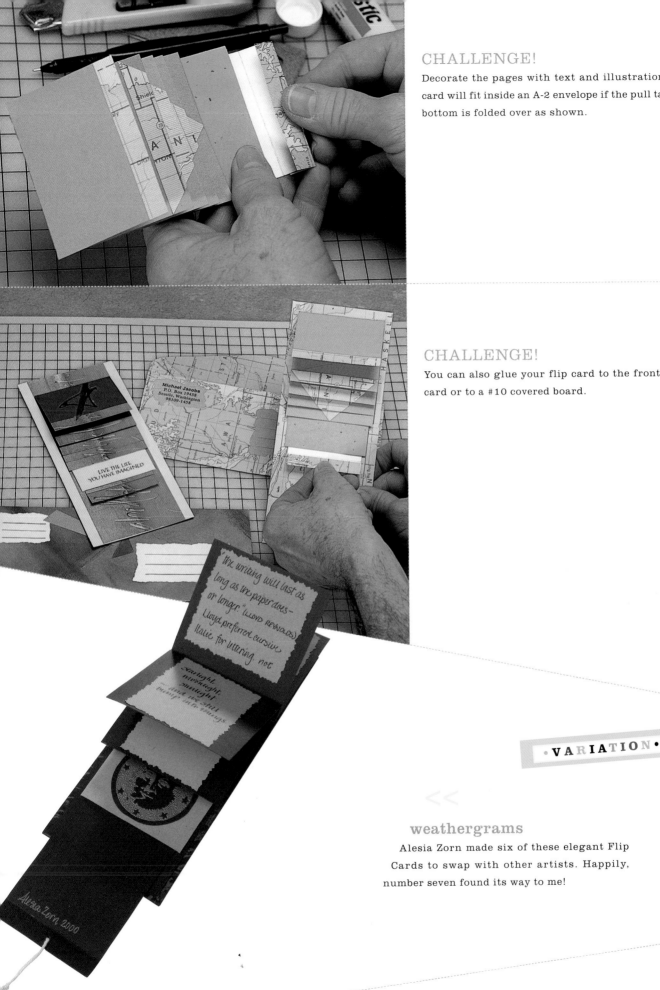

CHALLENGE!

Decorate the pages with text and illustrations. This card will fit inside an A-2 envelope if the pull tab at the bottom is folded over as shown.

CHALLENGE!

You can also glue your flip card to the front of a #10 card or to a #10 covered board.

· V A R I A T I O N ·

<<

weathergrams

Alesia Zorn made six of these elegant Flip Cards to swap with other artists. Happily, number seven found its way to me!

My original drawing for this card looked simple enough. I thought it would be a piece of cake to design an A-2 card based on my concept. Not so! This extremely "simple" card required numerous models before it worked, so I was a happy camper when I finally made the prototype for the card that follows. Here's my challenge to you once you understand the basic mechanism: Change the size and position of the windows to make an Around-the-Block Card to fit a #10 envelope. And remember, these cards can be oriented vertically, too!

around-the-block
card

materials >>

card > two 8½" x 4¼" (21.6cm x 10.8cm) pieces of cardstock (grain short)

component a pattern (page 93)

component b pattern (page 93)

basic tool kit (page 8)

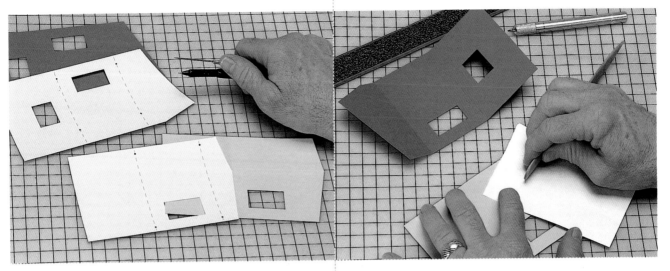

1 trace and cut out patterns

Trace the patterns for components A and B, including the windows, to the inside surface of two separate pieces of cardstock. Pierce holes through the four dots indicated on the patterns. Cut out both components, including the windows.

2 score, crease and fold components

Align your ruler with the pierced holes and valley score, fold and crease each component as indicated on the patterns. (For instructions, see pages 12–13.)

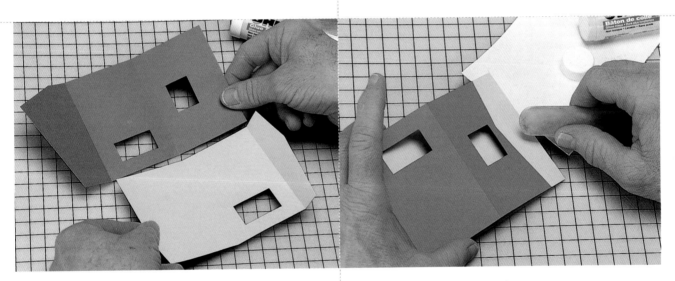

3 position components

Position the components with the flap on component A (the one with two windows) facing left and the flap on component B facing right, as shown above.

4 attach components

Flip component A over component B. Apply glue to the right inside flap of component B and fold it over component A. Make sure the right edge of component A is positioned in the fold of the flap, and that the sides of each component are flush. Burnish the flap.

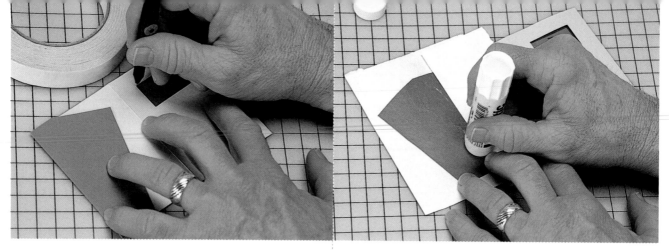

5 trace and number windows

Flip the unit over. Fold the left flap on component A to the right, over component B, and secure it temporarily with a small piece of double-sided tape. Trace the window on the right side of component B to the inside surface of component A and write the number 1 in the center. Hold down the fold on the left side of the card and rotate the card to the left. Trace and number windows 2 and 3. Rotate the card to the left again, trace and number windows 4 and 5. Rotate the card to the left a third time, trace and number window 6.

6 walk around the block

Open the card to reveal the traced and numbered windows. Add text inside the windows in proper numerical order and erase all remaining pencil lines. Or, if you prefer, write on paper rectangles slightly larger than the windows and glue them over the boxes in the proper order. Close the card, hold the large flap in place, and "walk around the block" to make sure your words are in the proper sequence. Apply glue to the large flap, using glue guards to protect areas you do not wish to glue, and burnish to component B.

· VARIATION ·

to judy, with love

Around-the-Block Cards can be made in any size. This #10 card is designed to move back and forth. Half-images cut into the folds become whole and frame the hand-written text when the receiver works his or her way "around the block."

>>

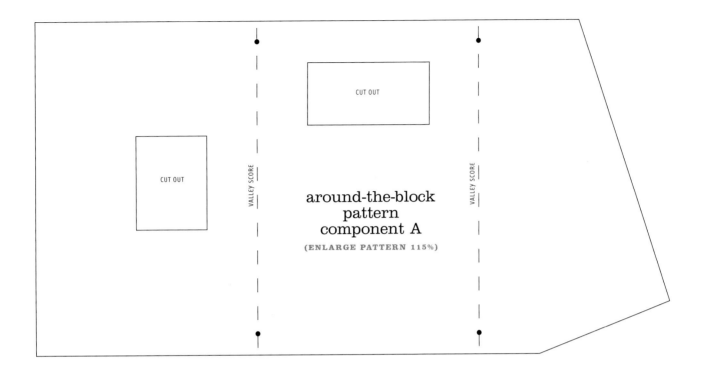

CUT OUT

CUT OUT

VALLEY SCORE

VALLEY SCORE

around-the-block pattern component A

(ENLARGE PATTERN 115%)

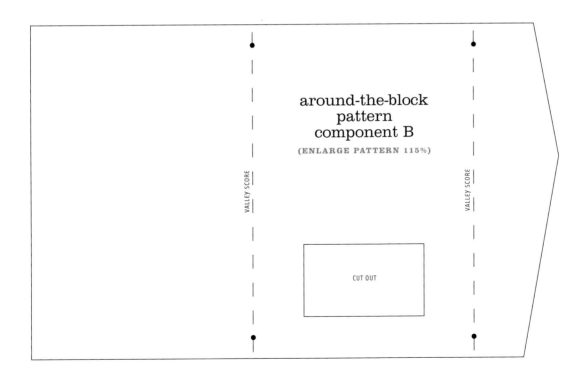

VALLEY SCORE

VALLEY SCORE

around-the-block pattern component B

(ENLARGE PATTERN 115%)

CUT OUT

resources

Below is a list of recommended magazines, periodicals and manufacturers of cardmaking supplies. See your local retailer to purchase the supplies in this book.

magazines and periodicals

RubberStampMadness
Phone: (541) 752-0075
Email: rsm@rsmadness.com
Web site: www.rsmadness.com
> Stamping arts and crafts magazine

Somerset Studio/
The Stampers' Sampler
Phone: (877) STAMPER
Web site: www.somersetstudio.com
> Bimonthly sister publications featuring stamping information and projects

Umbrella
Phone: (310) 399-1146
Email: umbrella@ix.netcom.com
Web site: www.colophon.com/journal
> Book and mail art news and reviews worldwide

manufacturers and suppliers

Clearsnap, Inc.
Phone: (800) 448-4862
Email: contact@clearsnap.com
Web site: www.clearsnap.com
> Inkpads, stamps and accessories

Creative Imaginations
Phone: (800) 942-6487
Web site: www.cigift.com
> Scrapbook papers and stickers

The Creative Zone
Web site: www.thecreativezone.com
> Papercraft, creativity and book arts workshops; papercraft kits

Daniel Smith
Phone: (800) 426-6740
Web site: www.danielsmith.com
> Art supplies and papers

Eckersley's Arts, Crafts and Imagination (Australia)
Phone: 1 (300) 657-766
Web site: www.eckersleys.com.au
> Arts and crafts supplies

Fiskars, Inc.
Web site: www.fiskars.com
> Straight and decorative scissors and paper cutters

Golden Paints
Phone: (607) 847-6154
Web site: www.goldenpaints.com
> Painting media, molding paste

John Neal Books
Phone: (800) 369-9598
Web site: www.johnnealbooks.com
> Art and calligraphy supplies, papers, tools and books

Marvy-Uchida
Phone: (800) 541-5877
Web site: www.uchida.com
> Markers, dye inks and supplies

Nasco Arts and Crafts
Phone: (800) 558-9595
Email: info@nascofa.com
Web site: www.nascofa.com
> Art materials and tools

Paper and Ink Arts
Phone: (800) 736-7772
Web site: www.paperinkarts.com
> Art and calligraphy supplies, papers, tools and books

Pearl Paint Co. Inc.
Phone: (800) 451-PEARL
Web site: www.pearlpaint.com
> Arts and crafts supplies, papers

Ranger Industries
Phone: (800) 244-2111
Web site: www.rangerink.com
> Inks and accessories

Silver Fox Stamps
Web site: www.silverfoxstamps.com
> Huge listing of rubber stamp stores

Stewart Superior Corp.
Phone: (800) 558-2875
Web site: www.stewartsuperior.com
> Stamp pads and accessories

Teri Martin Designs
Web site: www.terimartin.com
> Personally designed text and card-stock papers and acid free stickers (produced and marketed by Creative Imaginations)

Tsukineko
Phone: (800) 769-6633
Email: sales@tsukineko.com
Web site: www.tsukineko.com
> Stamp pads, pens and inks

Utrecht
Phone: (800) 223-9132
Web site: www.utrecht.com
> Art supplies

USArtquest, Inc.
Phone: (800) 200-7848
Web site: www.usartquest.com
> Art supplies

index

Try your hand at these other **fun crafts** with guidance from North Light Books!

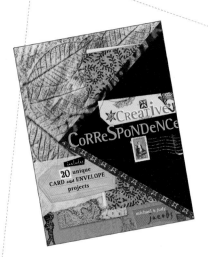

Creative Correspondence

You can create spectacular decorative mail with help from **Creative Correspondence**! You'll find 20 step-by-step projects including letters and envelopes with photo inserts, stapled booklets, acetate address windows and clever self-mailers. With the techniques demonstrated inside, you'll achieve great-looking results from start to finish.

ISBN-13: 978-1-58180-317-4, paperback, 96 pages, #32277
ISBN-10: 1-58180-317-6, paperback, 96 pages, #32277

Bright Ideas in Papercrafts

Bring a personal touch to every celebration, holiday and special occasion with **Bright Ideas in Papercrafts**. Inside, you'll learn to make 23 elegant projects using all of your favorite tools, from decorative edging scissors to paper crimpers, archival papers and more. It's easy, fun and fast! Start creating handcrafted keepsakes that will be treasured for years to come.

ISBN-13: 978-1-58180-352-5, paperback, 128 pages, #32325
ISBN-10: 1-58180-352-4, paperback, 128 pages, #32325

Simply Beautiful Greeting Cards

Perfect for all papercraft enthusiasts and crafters, **Simply Beautiful Greeting Cards** features 50 cards, each designed to be made quickly and easily, plus variation ideas for more inspiration. You'll also learn how to add simple and elegant touches with ribbon, charms and well-placed images. Every card includes easy-to-follow instructions and can be made with inexpensive materials available in any craft store.

ISBN-13: 978-1-58180-564-2, paperback, 128 pages, #33019
ISBN-10: 1-58180-564-0, paperback, 128 pages, #33019

These books and other fine North Light titles are available from your local art & craft retailer, bookstore, or online supplier.